Practical Gardeners' Guides

THE FLOWER GARDEN

Arthur Billitt

CONTENTS

NOTES
For convenience, ease of growing symbols have been incorporated in the A – Z sections.
They can be interpreted as follows:
   *Easy to grow plants
  **Plants which require more than average care
***Temperamental or difficult to grow plants
These symbols are appropriate provided the soil is
suitable and fertile.

Published in 1987 by Octopus Books Ltd,
59 Grosvenor Street, London W1

© Cathay Books 1984
ISBN 0 7064 2588 X

Printed in Hong Kong

GUIDELINES FOR SUCCESS

STARTING FROM SCRATCH
The perpetual hurry of life tempts most of us to start seed sowing or planting out bedding plants into the flower garden before the ground has been thoroughly and properly prepared. This is a sure way to disappointing results.

If you are starting with a brand new garden plot, the first thing to do is to remove all rubble and builders' waste, which, if left on the soil, soon turns it sour. Then you must plan the garden lay-out. Remember that few flower gardens are complete without a lawn, but just where you site it will inevitably affect the position of the flower beds, and therefore, ultimately how much or how little sunshine the flowers themselves will receive. North- and east-facing beds will always be less successful than those that face south and west because they are that much colder.

THE RIGHT TOOLS FOR THE JOB
I am a great believer in lightweight, but strong garden tools. The heavier the tools, the more energy is required to use them. The principal tools that a flower gardener needs are a spade and fork for digging the ground, incorporating compost and manure, lifting plants etc., a cultivator for knocking down the clods of earth in the spring and a rake for raking over the ground to make it even and level, ready for sowing or planting; a little fork and trowel for planting out, a hoe and a border fork for controlling weeds and a good pair of secateurs.

My spade must have a thin blade and a wooden shaft. I would not buy a stainless steel one; the stainless steel is a visual luxury that increases the weight. Spades are of course, made in several sizes; never buy one that is too big for your particular manpower on the assumption that you will cover the ground more quickly with it. Many have tried, only to suffer disappointment and backache.

The cultivator I favour is three-pronged with broadened ends to the tines. Again it is lightweight so it really requires very little energy on my part to use. In addition to this long-handled one, short-handled versions are available, generally intended for use by the physically handicapped or by children. I find them most useful in closely planted areas.

The secret of success in preparing seed-beds is to get a really fine tilth, and this is where the rake comes into its own. I like one with a 30-cm-(12-inch-) head. For dealing with those weed seedlings, again with as little effort as possible, I use a dutch hoe. This implement can be bought with various widths of blade; a very wide one is not really suitable for use in flower borders. Instead select one with a 13 cm (5 inch) wide blade. For use in the herbaceous border and amongst roses, I find a border fork most valuable, particularly for loosening obstinate weeds. Mine has a wooden handle and good sturdy tines.

For pruning roses or cutting down herbaceous plants at the end of the season, you will need a pair of secateurs. Make sure they fit comfortably into your hand, are not too heavy to handle and are sufficiently strong and sharp to make a good, clean cut.

SOIL TYPES
Soils vary greatly both from the kind of earth of which they are comprised and their mineral content. Whilst it is not necessary to analyse your soil minutely, it is important to understand its properties otherwise you will not know which plants will grow happily.

Basically the differences in soil types are related to the ratio of sand and clay in their make-up. Increases in the sand content makes the soil lighter and more porous. It warms up quickly, but also dries out more quickly, and it tends to be quite short of nutrients. Addition of organic material such as compost or peat helps to retain moisture in the soil and gives it more substance. Clay soils, with low sand content, tend to be wet and cold early in the season. Winter digging, with the clods left rough to weather, makes the preparation of the soil in spring easier and also improves the drainage. Work in some well-rotted compost or manure while doing the winter digging. Once a clay soil has been well cultivated and plants have become established in it, they will grow well, for it is very fertile.

Digging with the right weight spade (top) and preparing the seed bed with a rake

Using a long-handled cultivator (top) and weeding with a dutch hoe

Garden soils may be acid or alkaline and you can discover which yours is by checking on the plants that are growing (if the garden is already established) and then looking up what conditions they favour. By and large a chalky soil has a high alkaline content, clay soils tend towards alkalinity and sandy soils have a higher acid content. Soil with a high acid content can be corrected with applications of garden lime, while digging peat into alkaline soils will help to redress the balance. However, bear in mind that you cannot change this aspect of your soil for ever; you have to repeat the applications regularly or the soil will merely revert back to type. If it is not too overtly one way or the other, it is generally better to live with the overall soil, and then if you want to grow plants that are really not happy with the prevailing conditions, you can treat the soil individually for them.

PREPARING THE FLOWER BEDS
All digging is best done in the late autumn or

winter when the heaviest clay soils particularly benefit and can be made easy to work if the turned over clods are exposed to the winter elements. The water within them freezes, splitting them open. When you are digging, it is a good idea to incorporate some well-rotted garden compost or manure into the bed to enrich it. In the spring, it is then a comparatively easy job to attack the turned over clods with the cultivator and knock them down into smaller lumps. A work over with the rake will give an acceptable tilth for seed sowing or planting. Lighter soils can be dug in the spring without too many problems, but again, it is really better to dig them over in the autumn. If you were to dig a sandy soil in a dry spell in the spring, the loss of moisture incurred as the soil is turned over may well cause it to become excessively dry, thereby increasing the need for artificial watering later.

It is during this deep digging operation that you want to make sure you remove the roots of all perennial weeds such as couch grass, thistles, docks, nettles and the like. Annual weeds can be dealt with later on when they start emerging as little seedlings (see page opposite).

FERTILISERS – FEEDING AND MULCHING

There are few flowers and plants that do not benefit at some time or another from a little additional feeding. In many instances, this can be applied to the ground before planting – for example when planting herbaceous plants sprinkle some bonemeal or general fertiliser into the planting holes. Alternatively feed plants during their growing season.

A balanced garden fertiliser will contain ingredients to supply the three major plant growth nutrients, which are nitrogen, phosphates and potash, plus, possibly trace elements such as iron, magnesium, manganese etc. Organic fertilisers based on natural ingredients are usually more expensive and somewhat slower in action than inorganic ones, but are still preferred by some people. Both inorganic and organic fertilisers are available as powders, granules or liquids. To avoid waste, never exceed the recommended dosage or dilution rates and wait until the winter rains have ended. Apply to the soil around the plants.

Fertiliser formulations for applying to the foliage – known as foliar feeds – are available.

They should be sprayed on the plant when the weather is cool – either in the morning or the evening. This approach to plant feeding can be valuable in an emergency when plants are under stress for some unusual reason such as long periods of dry or very hot weather.

Herbaceous plants and shrubs such as roses will also benefit from a spring 'mulch' which helps to preserve moisture in the ground, as well as helping to keep down weeds as they have to force their way up through the thick covering. Simply put a layer of peat, or compost round the base of the plants. It will soon be hidden as the new growth emerges.

COMPOST MAKING

Well-made, well-rotted compost is an invaluable component of the flower garden for when returned to the beds it helps to maintain fertility. It is important to make as much of it as you can even though, apart from lawn mowings and leaves there is not going to be a great deal of waste plant material to use for compost making in the flower garden.

We make our compost by a slow but sure method which takes about twelve months in all and costs virtually nothing. It is a simple procedure; put a 13-15-cm (5-6 inch) layer of green material directly onto the soil in the wired-in compost bin. On top of this put a sprinkling of garden soil (this supplies the necessary micro-

For a good compost, build up layers of waste sprinkled alternately with soil and garden lime

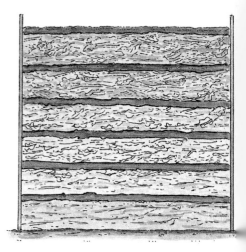

organisms which will work on the waste material) and then another 13-15-cm (5-6 inch) layer of vegetation waste. Top with a sprinkling of garden lime. From then on, repeat these layers until the compost bin is full. If you have no general waste material, but only grass, it would be wise to use a recycler which prevents the compost from becoming slimey. Your compost would then be ready after about six months.

FLOWER BED MAINTENANCE
Apart from feeding and mulching plants, two things are necessary to keep the flower beds in good condition – watering and weeding.

There will inevitably be times during the summer when some, if not all, your plants need your help if they are to get all the water they need. Start by making sure the ground in which you plant them is moist, and water the young plants as they are getting established in a new position. Thereafter, water as necessary, but do not wait until the plants start to wilt before giving them water as it could then be too late to achieve recovery. The best time to water is in the evening; this is when the plants derive the maximum benefit. If this is really not convenient, do it early in the morning, but never in the middle of the day when the sun is at its

Alyssum saxatile and Aubrieta

hottest. Do not just dribble water on the surface round the plant; that will only bring the roots to the surface and ultimately will cause more stress to the plants than giving them none at all. Make sure that the water goes right down to the roots by giving the ground a prolonged soaking. Bear in mind that once you have started watering established plants during a dry spell, you must keep on watering them regularly. By and large it is better to prepare the soil so that it is really moist and water-retentive.

It is obviously necessary to control the weeds in any flower garden, both so the plants are shown off to their best advantage and to ensure they do not suffer or become smothered. The secret of continuous weed control in any bed is to go round with a hoe regularly, starting as early as the beginning of March – to disturb the weeds before they have time to make any foliage or start seeding. An old saying among experienced gardeners is 'one year's weed seeding will save seven years weeding'.

It is important that the roots of some plants should be disturbed as little as possible (see in the A-Z listings), in which case you should weed round them by hand.

CULTIVATION AND ROUTINE CARE

CHOOSING THE RIGHT PLANTS

Success in gardening becomes so much easier when the plants you want to grow like both your soil and the climate that prevails in your area. Problems and disappointments occur when the desire to grow specific flowers is so strong that it causes one to disregard these two vital growing factors. Rhododendrons, azaleas and camellias are a case in point; they all like an acid medium, so to attempt to grow them on a chalky soil for example, would be asking for trouble – or a great deal of expense to try to overcome the problem by changing the basic nature of your soil.

There are few climates in the world where so many plants can be grown as here in the U.K., but as the winter frosts vary so greatly in intensity, the permanent planting of half-hardy subjects is generally unsuccessful, certainly in the colder areas. If you want to grow them and preserve them through the winter, be prepared to take care of them in one way or another during the winter (see page 14).

If you are new either to gardening or to your district and are therefore unsure just what will and will not flourish in your soil and climate, a peep over the fences down the road or a few visits to local gardens should answer your queries about what to plant initially. Experiments can come later. In selecting your plants, do make sure you site them carefully in relation to their need for full sunshine or partial shade. By doing so, you should be able to fill all the odd corners in the garden, thereby providing the maximum amount of interest and colour. Aim, too, to spread colour throughout the garden and choose plants that have varying flowering times so that you have a cheerful display from May to September. Try to get a good balance of shapes, mixing tall plants with those that are bushy, rather than putting all those with up-right growth habits together. Obviously you should put the tallest plants at the back of a bed, but avoid too many upright subjects, unless you are deliberately trying to give the effect of height. You will achieve a much softer overall effect by not planting your flowers in regimented straight lines.

GROWING YOUR OWN PLANTS

All sorts of plants are on sale at nurseries and garden centres in the spring under the heading of 'bedding plants'. Generally speaking, this is an expensive way to buy most plants, as clearly the nursery has done all the initial work and will be charging for their time. In any event, you will

have far more fun and achieve greater satisfaction in your gardening if you raise your own plants. This you can do either by growing them from seed, or by taking cuttings or small pieces of rooted material from established plants. Before we look at these various forms of propagation, though, a word about bedding plants, for they do have a place in many flower gardens. They are a way of getting colour quickly and safely into your flower beds and you can buy exactly what you want, in the numbers you want. As a general rule, do not buy these plants until well into May, so that with the danger of frost past, you can plant them out quickly. Many garden centres offer plants for sale far too early, with the result that if you plant them immediately, they will suddenly be killed off by a late frost.

A well organized greenhouse can be a tremendous help to the flower gardener

GROWING FROM SEED

Great numbers of plants can be raised from seed; depending on how hardy (i.e. ability to withstand cold and frost) the subject is, you can either sow seed outside or start it off indoors.

Outdoor cultivation

Seed of hardy annuals, hardy biennials and hardy perennials can all be sown straight into the ground outside. Hardy annual seeds can be sown where the plants are required to flower. The ground should have been dug in the autumn as recommended on pages 5-6, then broken up with a cultivator in the spring. The aim is to get the soil into a really fine, workable stage, so that it crumbles easily in your hand. Rake it over just prior to sowing to make sure you have a really fine tilth with no large stones or clods of soil on the surface. Then either broadcast the seeds over the ground or draw out shallow drills with the edge of the hoe or rake and scatter the seeds along these. The seeds of many annuals are quite small and it is important not to cover them with too much soil.

Always read all the directions on seed packets. You will find that mid-April is the best time to sow most hardy annuals, but do wait for good weather to get the right sowing conditions – that is a fine, dry top tilth with moist soil underneath.

When the seedlings appear and are large enough to handle, thin them out by pulling out the weaker ones.

The seeds of hardy biennials and perennials are more usually sown in a seed bed rather than straight into the place where they are intended to flower. This is because they will generally take some time to become established and it is more sensible therefore to fill the flower beds with flowering annuals in the meantime. Use a small patch of the garden as a seed bed; it should be in a light and sunny, but well-protected position. The soil should be in good condition – warm and full of nutrients. Rake it over to prepare it for seeds as you did the garden, to produce a fine tilth free from stones. It should be free from weeds as the seedlings may have to stay put for some long time before being transplanted. The procedure for growing these is the same as for hardy annuals; sow the seeds at the times recommended on the seed packets and thin out seedlings so that those you

ABOVE: *Sow seed in shallow drills (top) and thin out to leave the stronger plants*
RIGHT: *For indoor cultivation, sow seed in an electric propagator (top left) or in a seed tray (top right). Thin out to leave about 28 seedlings (bottom left). The plants can be hardened off in a cold frame (bottom right)*

want have sufficient room to grow unhampered. If the weather is dry, make sure that the seed bed is kept moist. Transplant the seedlings at the recommended times.

Indoor cultivation

All plants that are categorised as being half-hardy will need to be started indoors. The kitchen window sill can be a suitable site for seed trays, providing the house temperature does not drop dramatically during the night when central heating goes off. For raising seedlings on a small scale, it is probably worth investing in a small electric propagator. It should be fitted with a built-in thermostat which holds the temperature at 16°C (62°F). Even if you have a heated greenhouse, a propagator of this type will keep the heating cost down as there will be no need to heat the whole greenhouse. Again, read the directions on the seed packets to find out the right time for sowing, as this will vary considerably. Begin by filling the seed trays with a seeding compost (see page 13), which should feel moist. Sprinkle the seed over this and cover with another very fine layer of sifted compost. Keep the compost moist as the seedlings start coming up; you can speed up germination by covering the trays with polythene. Thin out the seedlings either by pulling out the weaker ones or by transplanting the tiny plants. This is known as 'pricking-out' and the important thing to remember is not to put too many seedlings into each seed tray. I find that 28 is about the right number for a standard tray and will give you good strong plants to transplant. Once in these trays, the seedlings must be placed in a good light (i.e. no longer in the propagator) otherwise they will soon become weak and drawn, but they must still be kept in a warm place. When the plants get too big for the trays, you should pot them into small individual pots filled with potting

compost (see page 13).

Before planting out into their flowering positions, they must be *hardened off*. This means getting them used to the climate gradually before they have to withstand it all the time. You can either put them in a cold frame (which should be in a sheltered position protected from cold winds) or you can put them out into the garden by day and bring them back indoors at night. Remember that if they are exposed to frost at this time, they will die.

Planting out
This should be done when all danger of frost has gone and the plants are healthy and well established. Make sure the compost around their roots is very moist, then dig a hole in the garden where you want them to be. Remove the plant from the pot and put it in the hole with as much of the growing medium around the roots as possible. If the soil is inclined to be dry, water the plants immediately in order to help them get established quickly.

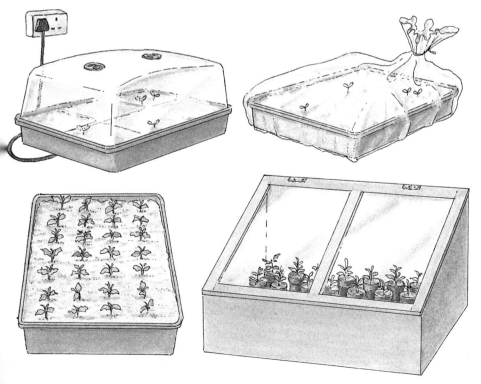

OTHER METHODS OF PROPAGATION

Although many perennials can be grown from seed, once you have the plant in your garden, you will want to propagate it by taking cuttings, by layering, or by dividing the roots to give 'rooted offsets'.

Taking cuttings

Some hardy perennials, such as lavender, can be propagated from non-flowering shoots taken during the late summer. You can either take a soft cutting or a heel cutting. The former is a cutting taken immediately below a leaf joint. For a heel cutting, remove the shoot with a heel of the harder stem from the parent plant. For both types, remove a few bottom leaves before dipping the cut end in a rooting powder or solution. The cuttings are then inserted into a pot filled with moist seed compost or into a special rooting bag. Place the pot or rooting bag into a plastic bag to prevent drying out. Make sure that the plastic does not rest on the cutting and remove it when rooting has taken place.

Chrysanthemums and dahlias can be propagated from cuttings taken during early spring. For this purpose the chrysanthemum stools (roots) or dahlia tubers are housed in warm conditions, ideally in a greenhouse, to produce young growth early. These young shoots are then cut off and potted into a pot filled with moist seed compost.

Without heat outdoor chrysanthemums and many other perennials can be propagated from root cuttings, that is, individual shoots removed from the stool with a few pieces of root still attached.

ABOVE: A soft cutting is taken immediately below a leaf joint

CENTRE: A heel, or semi-hardwood cutting is taken by removing the shoot with a heel attached to it from the parent stem

RIGHT: Dip the cut end of any cutting in a rooting powder or solution, then put the cuttings round the edge of a pot filled with moist potting compost. Cover with a plastic 'tent' to prevent the compost from drying out. Support the plastic with hoops of wire so that it cannot touch the cuttings, and remove it as soon as the cuttings have rooted

Pin down a shoot to be layered and cover with soil and a stone

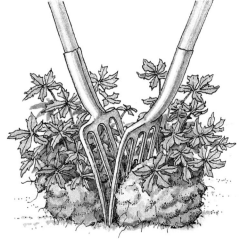

Divide a plant by using two forks placed back to back in the plant

Layering

Another propagation method, especially suitable for carnations and pinks, is layering. This involves pinning down a non-flowering shoot and covering it with soil. I often use a stone or piece of tile to hold the shoot down. The layered shoot is left attached to the parent plant until well rooted. It is then cut off and planted.

Division of plants

This is suitable for most perennials, and is best carried out in late March/early April when the plant should just be moving into new growth, so that the risk of failure with the rooted offsets is minimal. Dig the plant right out of the ground, then place two forks back-to-back in the plant and carefully prise it into pieces. Select the best young outside rooted pieces for planting straight back where you want them. Discard the older central root material.

SEED AND POTTING COMPOSTS

A special type of compost is needed for germinating seeds as tiny seedlings need relatively small amounts of plant nutrients until they have developed the root systems to cope with them and sufficient above ground growth to feed them. Later on the plants will need the higher nutrient levels of a potting compost.

Peat-based seed and potting composts are now more popular than those formulated with loam, the main difference between them being weight. Peat composts are much lighter and cleaner to handle but they do need more careful watering. Once a peat compost dries out it can be difficult to wet again to the right moisture level for either seedlings or plants.

All seed and potting composts tend to generate free nitrogen if stored for long periods. Free nitrogen in a compost can cause root damage so it is wise to buy from a supplier who has a rapid turnover.

CARE OF GROWING PLANTS

Besides the watering and feeding mentioned in the previous chapter, most flowers, perennials in particular, need some routine care if they are to achieve their full potential. Tall plants, for example, should be supported to protect them from being blown over in strong winds or battered down by heavy rain. Support them before any damage occurs, for once they have fallen over the stems will either break or bend so badly that permanent damage will be unavoidable. Support can be given by pushing canes, or a few pea sticks, into the ground around the plants and tying round the stems loosely with garden twine. In the case of single-stemmed

13

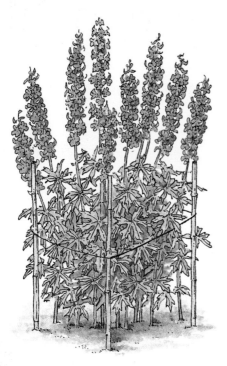

Support a clump of tall plants by pushing canes into the ground and tying twine loosely round canes and plants

very tall flowers such as sunflowers, secure to the support cane using a plant tie. Some bushy type plants can be supported merely by pushing twiggy sticks into the ground around them as they are growing. These will provide sufficient support without tying round them.

Many flowers, particularly those of biennials and perennials will flower more than once in a season if you pick or cut off the flower heads as soon as they have died. This is known as *dead-heading*. By removing the dead flower heads, you stop the plant putting its energy into making seeds and it can use it instead to produce more flowers. If you want to collect seeds to sow, then you must leave the flower heads to ripen into seed heads.

Apart from roses (see page 68), pruning is not a big activity in the flower garden. The pruning generally takes the form of cutting the stems of perennials right back down to the ground in the autumn so that they are clean and tidy.

OVERWINTERING

Hardy perennials that are to stay in their positions in the flower beds or herbaceous border through the winter need very little care. At the end of their flowering time, when the foliage has also begun to die back, cut them right down to the ground so that no more than 5 cm (2 inches) of stem is showing above the soil. Clear away all dead foliage from the ground around them leaving it really clean. This makes sure that there is no waste material to rot around the plants, nor is there a potential breeding ground for insects.

Tender plants are adversely affected by excessive wet and very low temperatures during the winter. A sheet of raised glass over a small plant, or a blanket of loosely tied bracken or straw around a larger plant goes a long way to ensure their survival. Plants which die down completely such as fuchsias can also be covered with a layer of bracken or straw to protect their roots from frost.

Some plants which grow from tubers, corms, rhizomes or bulbs may need lifting and storing in a dry, airy, frost-free building through the winter. Lift them in the autumn, shake off the soil and store.

A small, tender plant can be protected from excessively wet or cold weather by placing a raised sheet of glass over it

In this very colourful garden, exceptionally effective use is made of different sizes and types of containers filled with a profusion of flowering plants

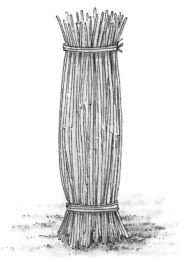

Make a 'blanket' of loosely tied straw or bracken to enclose a large, tender plant completely for protection from winter weather

CONTAINER FLOWER GARDENING

A patio or small paved area can be an attractive and colourful part of the flower garden, provided the plants are tended properly. Most plants can be grown successfully in pots and containers, but you must give them all the care and attention they will inevitably need.

Plants grown in containers can provide bright splashes of colour and interest and it is also an excellent way of being able to have those plants in your garden that do not like your type of soil. The smaller varieties of rhododendron, azalea and camellia are ideal subjects for growing in pots or containers provided these are filled with lime-free compost. Remember you must feed and water container-grown plants even in rainy weather, as most of the compost will be covered by foliage.

15

COMMON PESTS AND DISEASES

Whilst it is true that there are many garden pests and diseases and that some of them are fairly common, this need not be of great concern or worry to the amateur gardener. The secret of success in the fight against all of them is a watchful eye and a little basic know-how about the envioronment and the weather that encourages them. I would suggest a careful and observant daily walk round the garden, during which, with a sharp eye, you will soon spot any insect damage. You will quickly recognise, too, insects that feed on the sap they suck from the leaves, making a mess of the plants generally.

Sucking insects such as aphids (greenfly etc.) first appear almost singly on a plant, but if left undisturbed they multiply at a terrific rate and the plant becomes virtually 'lousey' in a few days. Hence on sight of the first one or two, take immediate action with an appropriate insecticide to eliminate them before too much damage is done. Generally speaking, sucking insects

Greenfly on rose shoot (1), leafminer on chrysanthemum (2), capsid bug on dahlia (3), narcissus fly (4)

are killed by skin absorbtion of the insecticide (a contact insecticide) whilst caterpillars are eliminated by digesting the sprayed insecticide.

In the case of diseases on plants it is somewhat different as once fungus diseases are established it is too late to affect a complete cure. Most plant diseases invade with little or no warning; by the time you have noticed them, they are established and the damage will have been done. Preventative spraying is therefore essential and must be done at the right time according to the manufacturer's directions for the fungicide you are using. Take notice of any disease problems in your garden as they occur and then take action against them next year.

COMMON PROBLEMS ON FLOWERS
Anemone: Both the DeCaen and the St. Brigid anemones are, on occasion, subject to attack by aphids (greenfly). They effect their damage by sucking the sap out of the young leaves. In addition, caterpillars and cutworms occasionally chew the buds, leaves and stems. Simple and safe control for all the pests is an insecticide based on two vegetable ingredients, potenone

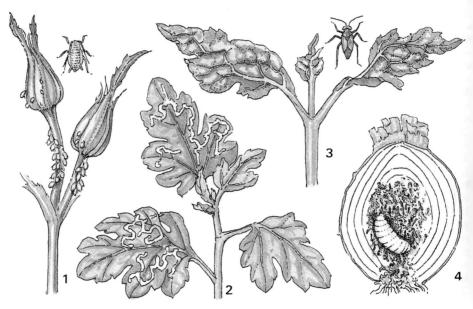

(the active ingredient of derris) and quassia (made from tree bark). Grey mould (botrytis) may cause rotting of flowers and buds early in the season particularly if the weather is wet. Prevention is the best idea; spray on a dry day with a product based either on carbendazim or thiram.

Anthirrhinum: Sucking insects of various types can cause leaf distortion and stunting of the growth here. Immediate action is advisable; spray with dimethoate and permethrin. Never use a fungicide based on malathion as anthirrhinums are very sensitive to it. Downy mildew disease which curls the leaves can be prevented by spraying with a fungicide based on thiram. Anthirrhinum rust is sometimes a problem in the south of England and is more difficult to control. Growing rust-resistant varieties is the best solution to the problem.

Asters: Attacks by aphids (greenfly) are very common and occur almost immediately after the asters have been planted out in the spring. The attack causes the leaves to curl up and the plants receive a considerable check in growth. Another pest is the capsid bug which punctures the leaves, thereby distorting them. As a preventive to both, spray with malathion a few days after planting out. Losses from foot rot disease also often occur soon after planting. To guard against it, water the ground with cheshunt compound solution. Never plant asters on the same spot two years in succession.

Begonias: Powdery mildew, which causes white powdery spots or patches on the leaves and stems, can be a problem but will only occur when the weather is continually cold and damp. At the first sign of such trouble, spray with a fungicide based on thiram and repeat at weekly intervals.

Chrysanthemums: Several sucking insects, such as aphids, capsid bugs and leaf miners, attack outdoor chrysanthemums. Leaf miners inject their eggs into the leaves and on hatching, the larvae burrow disfiguring trails through the leaves. Earwigs can also be troublesome. All these insects can be controlled with an insecticide based on HCH. Grey mould (botrytis) is a moist, warm weather problem causing damage to the blooms. Remove any affected blooms, then spray the plants with a thiram based fungicide which will also prevent powdery mildew.

Daffodils (all narcissi bulbs): The most serious

Blackspot and powdery mildew on rose (top) and antirrhinum rust

problem stems from the narcissus fly laying its eggs in May or June in or near the holes left by the dead foliage. The hatched larvae then tunnel into the bulbs, resulting in serious flower reduction (blind bulbs) and actual loss of bulbs. To reduce the risk of this egg-laying, remove the foliage just before it is completely dead, hoe or rake the surface to fill the holes, then water the area with an HCH insecticide. If the bulbs are later lifted for replanting discard any with soft necks. After replanting repeat the HCH insecticide treatment over the planted area.

Dahlias: These popular flowers are subject to attacks by aphids (blackfly particularly), capsid bugs, caterpillars and earwigs. We use a combined formulation of HCH, derris and thiram as a spray, which not only controls the pests but also prevents disease problems such as grey mould (botrytis). A simple earwig trap can be made by placing a 8 cm (3 inch) flower pot filled with dried grass upside down on top of the support stakes. Deal with the earwigs hiding in the pot each morning by holding the inverted pot above a bucket of hot water and tapping it.

Delphiniums: Greenfly can be a problem, but it is powdery mildew which coats the leaves and stems that is far more serious and it is liable to break out at any time during the season. Prevention is better than an attempted cure. Start early in the season whilst the plants are still small, by spraying with a combined spray of carbendazim and dimethoate plus permethrin. Both of these are systemic, and if sprayed at three weekly intervals will keep delphiniums clean. If powdery mildew is a recurrent problem, an application of garden lime and super phosphates early in the year should help to reduce the scale of the trouble.

Dianthus (carnations, garden pinks, sweet williams): Two forms of aphids can attack these outdoor plants. One sucks the sap from the leaves and causes stunted growth and distortion; spray with malathion immediately the pest is sighted. (The same spray will control thrips and carnation fly, the latter tunnels into the leaves and stems.) The other aphid infests the roots and is more difficult to control. The first sign is generally wilting during a dry spell, in which event drench established plants with an insecticide based on dimethoate. In the warmer and dryer parts of the country, carnation rust may occur starting first on the lower leaves as brown spore clusters. A fungicide based on thiram repeated at ten days intervals will keep the young foliage reasonably clean.

Gladioli: The most dreaded pests here are thrips – very tiny insects which suck the sap from the stems and leaves, turning them streaky and, finally brown. The pests will also feed on the flowers, making white flecks appear in the petals. Spray as soon as possible with an insecticide based on HCH. If the corms are lifted for replanting in the spring, dry them off very quickly but store at a temperature slightly below 10°C (50°F), otherwise the thrips will multiply on the corms. To control any aphids and caterpillars spray as for dahlias.

Hellebores: Early in the season white fly may appear in quantity on the flowers and foliage. Spray regularly from then on with dimethoate and permethrin until about the middle of June.

Leaf spot disease can disfigure the flowers and cause large black patches on the leaves. Remove and burn infected leaves and flowers, then spray with a liquid copper fungicide.

Hollyhocks: Rust has become a serious problem in many areas on established plants and no fungicide has yet been found to control it effectively. The raising of new plants each year and preventive spraying with a thiram based fungicide from seedling stage onwards is currently the only answer.

Irises (Flag Irises): At Clack's Farm, we have found leaf spot disease to be a constant problem. It starts in the spring with brown, oval-shaped spots which quickly enlarge, badly damaging or completely killing the infected leaves. Repeated applications of a fungicide based on carbendazim or buprimate and triforine may control it. The incidence of the disease is related to the local climate; in the southeast where it is drier it may not be a problem.

Michaelmas Daisies: Few plants are more prone to powdery mildew than Michaelmas daisies but with the new systemic fungicides it is possible to control it, providing preventive spraying starts well ahead of the first signs of the disease. Spray with a fungicide based on carbendaxim at fortnightly intervals. Should there be any sign of insect damage, change to a fungicide containing HCH and thiram. This will then control sucking and leaf-eating insects as well as controlling disease.

Pansies: A race of very small aphids attack pansies with deadly consequences. However, a routine spraying programme with malathion will prevent disaster. Stem rot disease can cause losses after planting out, but can be deterred by sprinkling 4% calomel dust in the planting hole. I have found that planting on fresh ground each year is the best insurance.

Petunias: There are no real pest problems but on some soils foot rot disease may occur. This too, can be reduced by planting on a different site each season. Where this is not possible, pre-planting watering of the soil with cheshunt compound solution does help to reduce losses.

Polyanthus and Primroses: A minute pest, the bryobia mite can cripple the plants, as can the red spider mite, too. Both pests deplete the foliage of sap and when this happens the plants are soon in serious trouble. Spray early with an insecticide based on dimethoate and permethrin or malathion.

Roses: The pests on roses are numerous – aphids (greenfly) caterpillars, leaf hoppers, thrips, sawfly larvae, etc. One or another is bound to turn up sometime during the growing season. To make sure that none escape, when they do arrive I use dimethoate and permethrin as an insecticide because it is effective against both the sucking and the leaf-eating insects. It maintains its effectiveness for about three weeks. In listing the diseases, black spot must be number one and it is widespread, especially in the cleaner air areas. The first symptoms appear as black spots in the older leaves; as the season progresses so does the extent of the disease, bringing about early leaf fall. It is this that depletes the health of the roses and unless some steps are taken to control the disease matters go on from bad to worse. The action I take is as follows; regular collection of infected fallen leaves because, although partially decayed, in the spring they release spores of the disease and so spread it still farther afield. I skim the soil with a spade so that the remaining debris gets buried, and prune the bush roses before Christmas instead of the third week in March, spraying them after pruning with a liquid copper fungicide. Thereafter, I repeat the spray treatment in early March when the buds are swelling and during the season I add carbendazim systemic fungicide to the insecticide spray. This is not only an additional aid in the battle against black spot but also excellent for the prevention of mildew.

In the south where the summers are warmer and drier, rose rust with its orange coloured postules occurs – the postules turn brown later in the season. Repeated spraying with thiram beginning in early spring as a preventive measure can be recommended.

Wallflowers: These are members of the cabbage family, so when the seed is sown during the summer it is wise to sprinkle bromophos in the seed drills to prevent cabbage root fly maggots feeding on the roots of the seedlings.

SLUGS AND SNAILS

At certain times of the year, especially in wet spells, both slugs and snails can do a lot of damage. Careful use of slug baits will reduce the populations but these are generally poisonous to domestic pets. An alternative way of

A simple earwig trap (top), see under Dahlia; and a slug trap

killing this pest is to sink a plastic container level with the soil, fill it with beer and put a large leaf over it. Empty it in the morning and repeat daily until you catch no more slugs in it. Far more important, however, is to remove the slugs' living quarters which may be areas of accumulated rubbish, uncontrolled vegetation, slabs of stone – in fact any hiding place where the conditions are cool and damp.

SOIL PESTS

All soil houses many insects, some of which are friendly and some harmful. Generally speaking the ones that move quickly are the gardeners' friends as they feed on other soil insects. The slow movers are the ones that stay put to feed on plant roots and stems. Usually you can leave well alone, but if you notice a real infestation in the soil, water it with a dilute HCH insecticide.

THE FLOWER GARDENER'S YEAR

The growing season from March to September will always be the busiest time for the flower gardener, but October to February should not be an inactive or uninteresting period of the year. It is during these five months, when the weather is occasionally kind, that the autumn clearing up, the winter digging, any alterations to the lay-out of the garden, rose planting, etc. are best carried out. These shorter day activities maintain the flower garden in good condition and incidentally, also keep the gardener fit.

January: Time to finish winter digging. The workability in the spring of the heaviest soils will be improved if the frost is allowed to get into the turned-up clods. Such digging also reduces slugs by exposing their eggs.

February: Usually the coldest month of the year but if it turns mild you could plant roses. Finish tidying up the herbaceous border by cutting down all dead stems; apply a light dressing of general fertiliser before lightly forking the soil, without disturbing any roots, between the plants. Sow begonia and geranium seed in a heated propagating frame.

March: With the ground well prepared and reasonably dry, this month could be the best time to plant herbaceous subjects and roses without the risk of losses. Remove the dead leaves from bearded irises and apply a general fertiliser to the ground about them, very lightly forking it in without disturbing their roots. Prepare a plot in full sun for dahlias; they will love it if it has been deeply dug with some well-rotted compost well beneath the surface to hold the moisture. Increase snowdrops now by lifting them complete with green foliage, then dividing and replanting them. Lily bulbs can be planted now, the fresher they are the better (see also September). Towards the end of the month is a good time to plant gladioli corms; if you put them 15-20 cm (6-8 inches) down they will probably survive next winter's frosts without lifting. They will also stand up to the winds better without extra support. It is time to give roses their first application of a balanced rose fertiliser. Sow half hardy annuals such as petunias, etc. indoors and remember they will need steady warmth for successful germination, so it is advisable to put them in a propagating frame.

April: Time to be out and about with the sprayer. If you have euonymus in the garden, begin by spraying this shrub as it is the host plant of overwintering blackfly. A regular inspection for the emergence of any aphids now will prevent major trouble later on. This is the month when annual weeds start to emerge and build up amongst the bulb foliage; hand weeding now will prevent seeding. Where there is less density of plants, start a weekly routine with the hoe. Even if the weeds have not yet emerged they will be in the white thread stage below the surface of the soil. Sow hardy annual seeds in the open but not before seed areas have been well prepared – made weed free and raked level to a reasonably dry fine tilth. Take care to sow evenly and thinly. Time to sow sweet-peas or plant out those raised under cover. Start hardening off petunias, marigolds, etc.

May: Keep on watching out for greenfly etc. particularly on roses and take action immediately when necessary. Add a systemic fungicide to the insecticide when spraying roses to prevent mildew. If the weather turns dry, any roses planted in March will appreciate a can of water in the evening. In the south, wait until the third week in the month before planting out begonias, petunias and other half hardy subjects. Farther north it is wise to delay still further until all risk of frosts have passed. If your soil is poor, a little garden fertiliser worked in before planting out will be a great help.

June: When you are spraying against greenfly do not forget that they may be breeding in the hedges around the garden, so spray them as well. Be particularly diligent with the hoe during dry and warm days; the sun then makes sure that the weeds die immediately they are up-rooted. Dead-head roses daily to ensure continuous flowering. Cut sweet-peas before the blooms start to fade; if allowed to set seed before cutting, the plants will soon cease to produce more flowers. Lift any daffodils you wish to move for re-planting later in the season, do not dry the bulbs in direct sunshine. Towards the end of the month, sow wallflower and sweet williams in shallow drills in a seed

bed for transplanting later. Remember the importance of watering young, recently bedded-out plants during hot dry spells.

July: By the middle of the month the first flush of roses will be nearly finished and it is time for another application of rose fertiliser after cutting each stem back to a strong outward facing bud. This is a good time to lift bearded irises if they have been down for three years or more. Select the strongest, single-rooted rhizomes for re-planting (if possible on a fresh site), but give the ground an application of a general fertiliser first. Remove the dead flowers from lilies unless you wish to save the seed. A good time to sow polyanthus and primroses outside in very shallow drills, preferably in a shady spot.

August: Herbaceous plants will need attention – dead-heading and general tidying. Take cuttings of border carnation, pinks, rock roses, etc., for rooting in pots, using a seed compost or a small rooting bag. Make sure that the cuttings are shaded and that the compost does not dry out. Take cuttings of your favourite roses.

September: Early this month, transplant wallflower and sweet william seedlings into a nursery bed or directly into the flower bed, depending on the space available. The move and extra spacing will encourage them to make bushy plants. Time to plant lilies – freshly lifted lily bulbs do best but beware of any showing signs of having dried out. Most lilies appreciate

Plan to have colour throughout the year

moist conditions but with good drainage and some dappled shade. During the month, clear away hardy annuals running to seed.

October: Take advantage of fine weather days to get rid finally of the residue of the hardy and half hardy annual bedding plants. Add all the debris to the compost heap. Early flowering and spray chrysanthemum stools will overwinter better if they are lifted towards the end of the month and put in a cold frame. After the first autumn frost, lift dahlia tubers and store them for the winter. Plant spring flowering bulbs.

November: Whilst the weather outside may not be too inviting this is the month for improving your garden soil. Whenever possible, dig it with a spade and leave it rough for the winter. Now is the best time to plant roses but do have the ground prepared ready for them.

December: Follow my example and prune your bush roses before Christmas. It is not yet time to put the spade away if there is still some open ground to be dug. When all is finished, the garden may look somewhat bare. An hour or two spent with a seed catalogue indoors and the posting of an order will make sure that you are indeed ready for next year, providing of course, that you have remembered to clean and oil your garden tools before putting them away.

Happy Gardening next year.

BULBS, CORMS AND TUBERS

For most of us bulbs are associated with the spring flowers, such as tulips and daffodils. If you choose carefully, however, it is possible to have a great variety of flowers from spring through summer to autumn, all grown from bulbs, corms or rhizomes.

There are a few golden rules when growing plants of this type. Always plant at the depth recommended by the suppliers, and find out, too, what kind of conditions – sun or shade – and the type of soil each individual likes. All bulbs need good drainage and the dead foliage should be quickly cleared away when the plant has finished flowering. If obeyed, these two rules prevent rotting of the bulbs and any build up of disease.

ALLIUM*

There are many different types of allium, or ornamental onion, some with flowering stems so tall that they need support to keep their flower-heads off the ground whilst others are sufficiently small to make them suitable for the rock garden. Planted amongst low-growing shrubs, the taller alliums make effective unusual displays. In common with all members of the onion family they appreciate well drained soil and as much sunshine as possible. Allium seed-heads are just as attractive as the flower-heads.

Allium aflatunense grows to 75 cm (2½ ft) tall, and with its large purple-lilac heads is exceptionally ornamental. It flowers in late May. *A. caeruleum* grows to 60 cm (2 ft) high and is widely available. It is a graceful plant with cornflower blue flower-heads carried on strong wiry stems. It flowers in June. *A. cowanii* grows to 60 cm (2 ft) high and has fine heads of pure white flowers which appear at the end of May. *A. moly* grows only to 30 cm (1 ft) high and is an old garden favourite. It has umbels of golden yellow flowers which appear in June.

Early autumn is the best time to plant all varieties. Once planted, leave them to multiply until the clumps become overcrowded. At this point, lift the bulbs and replant them separately. Sow seed outside in a seed bed immediately after it has ripened or, if you buy it, try to make sure it is as fresh as possible. Leave it for a season before pricking the seedlings out into a bed.

ANEMONE*

We grow *Anemone coronaria* from corms – the 'De Caen' and 'St Brigid' strains are selections that have evolved over the years to provide us with some of the most colourful of all early blooming flowers. Being natives of the warmer Mediterranean climate, they still need some special care and protection for quality and quantity flower production. In the south-western areas of Cornwall and Devon, they flower happily outside during the early months of the year, but elsewhere they will need protecting with cloches if they are to flower early. In all situations, plant in well-drained soil where there is plenty of sunshine. For spring flowering, plant the corms in September/October. The foliage will die down after flowering. Allow the corms to multiply without disturbance to give increased flowering in the following seasons.

'De Caen', the single flowered anemone, is usually offered as a mixture of brilliant colours but named varieties are available in separate colours. 'St Brigid' has semi-double flowers and is not quite so free flowering. Seed of both can be purchased for sowing any time, January to June, in a greenhouse or cold frame.

Among the small flowered varieties for rockery and wild gardens is the easy-to-grow *A. blanda* which reaches a height of 10-15 cm (4-6 inches) and has blue flowers that bloom in March/April. It is delightful and is even successful when planted in semi-shade. *A. blanda atrocaerulea* is another small one with lovely blue flowers. It increases rapidly after planting. Separate colours are available such as 'Charmer' – pale pink, 'Radar' – bright carmine and 'Splendour' – white. You can also buy these as a mixture.

BEGONIA**

Tuberous-rooted begonias need special care to get them into flower by planting-out time (June). For success, it is necessary to have a greenhouse, a propagating frame or some other facility with good light where the temperature does not drop below 18° C (65° F). Start the tubers in March by putting them hollow side uppermost in a moist peat compost. At this time, they can be spaced quite close to one another, but soon afterwards when growth starts, each plant will need a 2.5-cm (5-inch) half pot at least. Prepare the ground outside where you want them to flower by digging in some well-rotted compost or peat to hold the moisture. The plants will grow well in partial shade provided they are never short of water. For the best blooms feed with a liquid tomato fertiliser every fortnight. At the end of the season, after the first frost damage to the foliage, lift the tubers and dry them indoors. Store in a frost-free, airy place until March.

At Clack's Farm, we started with Begonia 'Non-Stop' mixed seed and raised plants from the seedlings in the greenhouse heated to 18° C (65° F). These we planted out in June. At the end of that season, we lifted the tubers and have since started them up into new growth, as explained above, each spring. The seed may be expensive but it is an investment in tremendous beauty. Most other varieties are only really suitable for greenhouses.

CHIONODOXA*
Commonly known as Glory of the snow, these early spring flowering bulbs, with their dainty small star-shaped flowers artistically arranged on

A beautifully coloured Colchicum speciosum

slender stems, are natives of the high mountains in Asia Minor. Plant them in the autumn in ordinary well-drained soil where they will be able to have a full view of the sun, and leave them undisturbed. They will multiply rapidly to be a sheer delight every year. Our *C. luciliae* with its vivid blue, white-centred flowers has just done this. *C. luciliae* 'Rosea' has pure pink flowers and can be recommended, as can *C. gigantea* with large pale blue blooms.

COLCHICUM**
Autumn flowering colchicums can be used to advantage in a shrub border or even in rough grass. The flowers are held on naked stems, and they do make an attractive splash of colour. Whilst the flowers themselves take up only a small space, the large leaves can smother nearby plants in the spring. They also look untidy before they die back. These are two good reasons why it is important to choose the planting site carefully. The best effect is obtained when the corms are planted in clumps in August/September

Lily of the Valley, Convallaria majalis

and are then left for years.

C. *autumnale* (sometimes called the Autumn crocus) is a European native, much appreciated by autumn visitors to France, particularly to the foothills of the Alps. Its crocus-like flowers are a soft rosy lilac. The dark rosy purple flowers of C. *cilicium* appear slightly later. C. *speciosum*, in its several forms, such as 'Album' – a white, 'Disraeli' – a deep mauve and 'Lilac Wonder' – a pinkish lilac with a white throat – is probably best for garden planting.

CONVALLARIA*
Lily of the Valley

This well-known plant is famed for its graceful sprays of perfumed, bell-shaped flowers. It grows rampantly with us in the shade of a stone wall where the sun is never able to dry out the soil. It can generally be established in partial shade or even out in the open provided the soil never completely dries out. To ensure the right growing conditions, prepare the ground by digging in a liberal quantity of well-rotted compost. The best time to plant is September/October; make sure that each crown is planted with the point upwards. When the bed becomes overcrowded – which it will do after some years – lift and replant the bulbs after replenishing the ground with compost. C. *majalis* is the standard white form. It grows some 15-20 cm (6-8 inches) high. C. *majalis* 'Rosea' has pink flowers but it can be less vigorous.

CROCOSMIA*

This is closely related to montbretia and indeed is often mistaken for a giant and improved form of it. Perhaps this is not altogether surprising as montbretia was one of its parents. It is a plant that needs sunshine to flower well – in shade it does no more than just survive – and it does best in a light well-drained soil. If grown in the north it would appreciate the shelter of a south facing wall.

We started with a few corms of C. *masonorum* which grows to 75 cm (2½ ft) and we now have several well established clumps. The richly coloured flame-orange flowers on arching stems make a superb display from July to September, and it is excellent for cutting, too. A newer variety, C. *Lucifer*, has even finer and more colourful flowers of an intense brilliant flame red. These appear in June/July, and the plant grows to 90 cm (3 ft).

The best time to plant is March. When the clumps become overcrowded lift and divide them, then re-plant if possible on fresh ground which has had some well-rotted compost incorporated.

CROCUS*

The 'heralds of the spring' – crocus will grow in any type of soil. While the large-flowered crocus may be the most spectacular, we should not forget the small-flowered species which flower in February/March. Try C. *chrysanthus* mixed; they will quickly multiply and give an increasing display as the numbers build up. The same can be said for the large-flowered varieties; we grow 'Queen of the Blues',

'Pickwick' – pearly grey with dark centres and striped dark lilac, 'Jeanne d'Arc' – snow white, 'Remembrance' – a large violet purple and 'Large Yellow'. The last one was raided by sparrows until we discouraged them by no longer feeding them! October/November is the best time to plant.

CYCLAMEN**

The hardy cyclamen, C. neapolitanum is an exquisite plant which flowers in the autumn long after its foliage has died down. The tiny pink or white flowers are perfect miniature cyclamen on slender stems. They are fascinating to watch as they seem almost to dance in a slight wind. There can be few more beautiful sights in any garden than masses of these delightful flowers in a low golden autumn sunlight

The exquisite, miniature Cyclamen neapolitanum

especially if they cover a large area under a beech tree.

The secret with these treasures is to plant the corms (slight depression upwards) in the late summer, barely covering them with soil. They prefer a well drained situation where they are not likely to suffer scorching from hot sunshine. From then on, hand weed around them carefully so as not to disturb either the corms or the seedlings (see below). In a few years, the cyclamen will have extended their territory considerably. Seed is available; sow it in a cool greenhouse any time from October to March. Plants grown in this way will probably start to flower in their second or third year.

DAHLIA**

These are half-hardy, tuberous rooted perennials which require a sunny position in rich fertile soil, that is moisture retentive and well prepared.

As all parts of the plant are frost sensitive, planting must be delayed until the risk of spring frost has ended; this means late May/early June. Dahlia tubers can be planted out but it is more advisable to use tubers that have been started off in the greenhouse. However, best results of all are obtained with rooted cuttings from forced tubers, started in a warm greenhouse and hardened off before planting out. These methods are for the various decorative and exhibition types, which vary in height from 45 cm – 1.8 metres (18 inches – 6 ft). All but the shortest varieties need staking and tying during the growing season. For mass bedding-out dahlias can be raised from seed in a temperature of 15° C (60° F). 'Chi-Chi' mixed has a considerable range of colours in flowers and foliage.

At the end of the flowering season, bury the tubers at least 30 cm (1 ft) deep under a thorn

hedge or beside a fence, where they should be safe from rotting and frost.

ENDYMION NON-SCRIPTA* Bluebell

Our native bluebell is wonderful when seen in the spring as carpets of blue in a country setting or in a wild garden. However, it is wise to think twice before planting bluebells in a border; they spread so rapidly, both by multiplication of the bulbs and by seeds, particularly if the soil suits them.

ERANTHIS**
Winter Aconite

The winter aconites, E. hyemalis, are one of our earliest and brightest spring flowers. A wonderful bright golden yellow colour, they are rather like large buttercups on short stems set in rings of leafy bracts. Grown in masses they are stunningly cheerful. Plant the nobbly tubers, in spring, not more than 5 cm (2 inches) deep, in small groups. If the soil is good and inclined to be moist, they will soon spread. Always hand weed the area; never use a hoe. Any disturbance will prevent tubers multiplying and spreading over a much larger area. Ideal for naturalising under trees.

FRITILLARIA**

There are two species within this group of hardy bulbs that are of particular interest to the gardener: F. imperialis (Crown imperial) and F. meleagris (Snake's head). Both do best in well-drained moist soils. They should be planted either in full sun or in slight shade, after which they should be left undisturbed for years. We mark

their growing area with canes so that we know just where they are as there is no visible growth above ground between July and January and the slightest damage to an emerging stem in February will mean loss of flowers. The bulbs are fleshy, easily damaged and must be planted as fresh as possible from August to October. Plant Crown imperials 15-20 cm (6-8 inches) deep and Snake's heads 10-15 cm (4-6 inches) deep. We have two varieties of Crown imperials, both of which grow to 90 cm (3 ft). They are 'Lutea Maxima' which has deep yellow blooms and 'Rubra Maxima' which has brick red flowers. The Snake's heads which are much lower growing at 25 cm (10 inches) high are C. meleagris mixed. They have charming drooping bell flowers in many variations of chequering. All flower in April.

GALANTHUS*
Snowdrop

The 'Fair Maids of Feburary', this is the first outdoor bulb to flower and no garden is complete without them. Whilst they will grow and succeed in moist soils, they do best in heavy loams with plenty of moisture. Left undisturbed they multiply freely until, if grown in a border, they may need lifting and dividing to maintain maximum flower production. The time to lift and replant snowdrops is a couple of weeks after flowering whilst the foliage is still green. If dry bulbs are bought they should be very fresh; plant them straight away.

There are numerous varieties; G. nivalis is the com-

mon snowdrop and is usually chosen for naturalising in the grass and in shade under shrubs. For open ground it is better to plant the large-flowered varieties, such as G. elwesii or G. nivalis 'Viridapicis' with its green-tipped petals. My favourites are 'Mr. S. Arnot' which has large single flowers and G. nivalis plenus with large double flowers.

GLADIOLUS*

All gladioli do best when planted in a sunny position where the soil has been well prepared. Some old compost or manure dug in also helps as does good drainage. The corms are frost sensitive so the time to plant is late March/April. The depth is important and always plant at least 15 cm (6 inches) or even deeper; then unstaked flower stems do not topple over and if you are prepared to take something of a risk, the corms can be left in the ground through the winter. If not planted as deep as this, the corms need lifting in the autumn. Dry them off quickly indoors and store in a frost free airy place.

In addition to the large-flowered varieties, the more dainty primulinus and butterfly types appeal to me.

HYACINTHUS*
Hyacinths

Once hyacinths have been planted and left undisturbed, they will flower without fail each spring although after several years the quality of the flowers does deteriorate. They prefer a medium soil with good drainage. We regularly plant out our forced 'Christmas' hyacinths, they recover quickly and will flower for several seasons afterwards without lifting.

IPHEION**
This bulb plant, with its grass-like foliage, flowers from March to May. Its single flowers have six petals and they measure 3-5 cm (1½-2 inches) across. They are carried on 15-20 cm (6-8 inch) stems. Ipheion are natives of Mexico, and as a result they need a sheltered position in sun or slight shade plus good drainage and plenty of humus. September/October is the time to plant. Do not allow the bulbs to dry out before planting. Ipheion 'Wisley Blue', which has large violet blooms is probably the best.

IRIS*
Amongst the many bulbous iris the best known is probably *I. reticulata* which grows 15-20 cm (6-8 inches) tall. It is often planted with good effect in rock gardens, and it produces its purple-blue flowers in February/March. The variety 'Cantab' is a lighter blue than 'J.S. Dijt' which is a near purple. *Iris danfordiae*, with its vivid yellow flowers, needs planting at least 12.5 cm (5 inches) deep to prevent the bulbs splitting up into non-flowering bulblets. The tall Dutch iris which grows 75 cm (2½ ft) high is excellent for cutting in June. If left undisturbed it will flower for years provided it too, has been planted about 12.5 cm (5 inches) deep. In fact, the same is true of the Spanish and English iris. All iris do best in a rich moist soil.

LEUCOJUM* Snowflake
These hardy bulbous plants,

The beautiful Lilium regale

with snowdrop-like flowers, do well in any garden soil, whether they are planted in sun or partial shade.
L. aestivum – grows 50 cm (20 inches) tall and in spite of its common name – Summer Snowflake – actually flowers in March/April. It has pure white bells on each stem. *L. vernum*, smaller at 15 cm (6 inches) tall, is the spring snowflake, and it flowers soon after the snowdrop. It requires a moist cool peaty soil. Plant bulbs in late summer.

LILIUM**
This is a very extensive family of hardy lilies and we are more than grateful that our Clack's Farm lime-free soil suits most of them. The lilies' soil requirements are good drainage but with moisture retention (achieved by digging in plenty of compost). The ideal situation is for the bulbs to be in light shade, but with the flower heads out into the sunshine. Flowering from June until August, we have several varieties, such as 'Pirate', 'Enchantment', 'African Queen', 'Green Dragon' and many

others. In July, we enjoy *L. regale*, which, with its yellow throated white flowers, is the easiest to grow. All these lily bulbs should be planted 15 cm (6 inches) deep as they are stem-rooted. The one we have to nurse most carefully is *L. candidum* (Madonna Lily). Plant this one with its 'nose' close to the surface and mulch with compost in spring.

All lily bulbs should be planted while they are as fresh as possible and you should allow them a few years to settle down. Sow seed immediately after harvesting in seed trays and keep outside in autumn.

MUSCARI*
Grape Hyacinth
These small, well-known bulbous plants thrive in a sunny position, in fact they multiply so rapidly that it is advisable to lift and replant the largest of

the bulbs each year. Plant in the autumn. *M. botryoides* 'Heavenly Blue' with sky-blue flowers is the best form. *M. botryoides* 'Album' is white.

NARCISSUS*
These are the hardy spring flowering bulbs which include the daffodils, jonquils and various species and hybrids. To many people the terms, 'daffodils' and 'narcissus' mean two different plants, but strictly speaking they are one and the same. All narcissi do well in most garden soils and a late summer planting allows the bulbs time to develop good root systems before the soil cools down. Our outstanding large golden-yellow trumpet daffodils include 'Golden Harvest' and 'Rembrandt' but there are long lists to choose

Nerine bowdenii is very colourful

from in the bulb catalogues. The superb 'Ice Follies' has attractive off-white flowers, and amongst the pure white, 'Mount Hood' is one of the best. We are also very fond of 'Fortune', which is a large-cupped variety with a reddish corona. Just some of the Narcissi varieties are 'Geranium', 'Cheerfulness', and 'Actaea'.

When you purchase bulbs make sure that the 'nose' of each bulb is firm. Plant early in the autumn and after flowering, let the foliage die naturally before cutting down.

NERINE**
Unfortunately only one species – *N. bowdenii* which grows 60 cm (2 ft) high – is hardy enough to be planted outside in this country. It requires a warm sunny position; ours does well in front of a south facing wall. It likes a light soil, particularly if given a summer mulch of well-rotted compost to supply nutrients. The foliage dies down during the summer and the large umbels of delightful pink flowers appear on naked stems in early autumn. Plant bulbs 10 cm (4 inches) deep in April.

RANUNCULUS*
Buttercup
R. acris 'Flore-pleno', the double yellow buttercup, which grows 75 cm (2½ ft) tall, is suitable for a herbaceous border provided it can have a position in full sun or half shade in moist soil. Other colours are available as a mixture. Plant the corms with their claws downwards in February March. To propagate, divide and then replant the corms in the spring.

SCILLA* Wild Hyacinth

This is another small bulbous plant that is well worth a place in any rock garden. It likes a well drained soil with a little added peat to hold the moisture. Its bell-like flowers appear in March.

There is a choice of several varieties; *S. siberica* 'Spring Beauty' which grows 15 cm (6 inches) tall and is a bright blue; *S. campanulata* mixed, taller at 35 cm (14 inches) and *S. tubergeniana* which has blueish-white flowers and grows only 10 cm (4 inches) high. Plant the bulbs as fresh as possible in late summer or early autumn. All are suitable for naturalising.

TRILLIUM* Wood Lily

The common name of this plant gives some indication of the growing conditions required – namely a moist soil, rich in humus and a position in light shade. *T. grandiflorum* (Wake Robin) grows 30 cm (1 ft) high and has short arching stems to carry its large three-petalled flowers that measure 5-7 cm (2-3 inches) across and appear in late spring. *T. undulatum* (Painted Wood Lily) grows 30 cm (1 ft) tall; its flowers have white petals that are reddish purple at the base and its coppery red foliage is an extra feature.

Plant the rhizomes as fresh as possible in late summer. Lift and divide them after the foliage has died down.

TRITONIA*

Closely related to freesia and Crocosmia, *Tritonia crocata* is somewhat less hardy, which is not surprising as it is a native of South Africa. In the U.K. it

The unusual flowers of Trillium grandiflorum

can only be regarded as a possible flower garden plant in the warmer areas. In those parts, it needs a light, well-drained soil and a sunny sheltered position. Its 60 cm (2 ft) spikes of bright orange flowers appear in May/June. Plant the corms in March for flowering a year later.

TULIPA* Tulips

Under this title there is the extensive genus of popular spring flowering bulbs with heights ranging from about 15 cm (6 inches) to 75 cm (2½ ft). Because of this variation, it is important to find out about the growth habit of the various types. Any good garden soil will suit tulips, but they like an open sunny position. While most hybrid tulips, such as the tall Darwins and May-flowering varieties,

deteriorate if left in the ground from season to season, some of the species persist well, and in fact, will multiply freely. For long-term planting, try *T. fosteriana* 'Madame Lefeber', which grows 45 cm (18 inches) tall and is a striking vivid scarlet, *T. greigii* 'Red Riding Hood', which grows 15 cm (6 inches) tall or *T. kaufmanniana* (Waterlily tulip) 30 cm (12 inches) tall. 'The First' is an exceptionally early variety and has pure white blooms tinted carmine-red on the reverse of the petals. It grows to 20 cm (8 inches).

To make your choice, I suggest you look through a bulb specialist's catalogue and order early so that you can plant in October.

ANNUALS

Annuals are plants that can be grown from seed to flower and die and in the same season. (HHA) in the text indicates that the subject is not completely hardy in our climate, consequently it is one that needs special treatment. Begonias, petunias and marigolds are good examples: their seed requires warm conditions early in the season for germination, and similar conditions to produce good plants, which are on the verge of flowering, towards the end of May, ready for planting outside when the risk of spring frosts is over. (HA) in the text indicates that the seed can be sown outdoors where the plants are intended to flower. There is a great variety within this group which means that with a few packets of seed it is possible to produce plenty of summer colour in the garden at little cost.

AGERATUM* (HHA)
Soft cushion-like flowerheads are the feature of this beautiful edging or bedding annual. Given a moisture-retentive soil and a sunny position it will flower from early summer until the first frosts. Water it if there is any danger of the ground getting dry and deadhead when the flowers die.

The height of the different varieties varies from 15-45 cm (6-18 inches). The taller varieties provide a useful cut flower. The colours also vary from a clear blue of 'Blue Mink' to bluish-mauve of 'Blue Blazer' and lavender blue of 'Blue Bouquet'. Sow in February/March under glass and keep at a temperature of 10-15°C (50-60°F) to germinate.

ALYSSUM* (HA)
This small ever-popular edging plant, Alyssum maritimum, is suitable for growing in the rock garden and in the crevices of paving or stone walls. It flowers continuously throughout the summer in any ordinary soil in a full sun position. It grows to a height of 10-15 cm (4-6 inches) and popular varieties are 'Little Dorrit' – white, 'Snowdrift' – white, 'Rosie O'Day' – pink and 'Royal Carpet' – purple.

Sow under glass in February/March and keep at 10-15°C (50-60°F). Sow in open ground in April/May.

AMARANTHUS* (HHA)
The red version of Amaranthus caudatus is commonly known as 'Love Lies Bleeding'. It is tall enough to grow in the centre of an annual bed or border. The flowers occur in long graceful tassels from July to October, and are ideal for cutting as they last well in water. The green variety 'Viridis' in particular is prized by flower arrangers. Other varieties include 'Crimson' and 'Tricolor Splendens'.

Amaranthus grow to 75-90 cm (2½-3 ft) and favour a sunny position. An ordinary soil is adequate but more impressive growth will result from planting in a deep rich soil. Sow under glass in March and keep at 15°C (60°F) or in March/May outside.

ANCHUSA* (HA)
Anchusa capensis is a biennial from which a strain has been developed for use as an annual. A good blue in the flower garden can be scarce at midsummer, but from July to August, anchusa can fill the gap with its large forget-me-not-like flowerheads of an intense blue. Sow seeds in March/May in open ground and transplant groups to the border. Growing to a height of 23 cm (9 inches), it is also ideal to grow in a container. A good variety is 'Blue Angel'.

ARCTOTIS*
African Daisy (HHA)
This grey-green leaved plant has large daisy-like flowers which come in a wide range of both pale and bright colours from late June until the first frosts. Some flowers have zones of contrasting colour towards the centre making them particularly striking. A good choice for a dry sunny position, after planting out, pinch out the growing tips at about 15 cm (6 inches) to encourage branching and cut or dead head after the blooms have died to encourage further flowering. They grow to a height of 30-75 cm (1-2½ ft), and the taller varieties may need some twigs for support.

Arctotis makes an attractive if short-lived cut flower. Sow in February/March under glass and keep at a temperature of 10-15°C (50-60°F).

BEGONIA SEMPERFLORENS** (HHA)

This is a fibrous-rooted begonia. Grow it as an annual, then at the end of the season lift the plants and pot them for further flowering indoors. The germination and early stages of growing are not the easiest but by planting-out time this begonia is generally a real survivor. The fleshy leaves help it through dry spells and it is equally at home in sun or light shade. Even deeper shade does not suppress it altogether. Plant it in the front of a border, or in any sort of container. It varies in height from 15-38 cm (6-15 inches). Masses of small flowers in shades of red and pink through to white are produced from June until the first frosts. The foliage may be green or bronze.

There are many seed mixtures which achieve a complete carpet of colour. Recommended varieties are 'Happy Choice', which has large flowers, 'Organdy' – mixed, 'Danica' – mixed, or available in individual colours of red, rose and scarlet, 'Ambra' – in various single colours, and 'Picotee' – white edged pink. Sow under glass from January to March and keep at a temperature of 20-25°C (68-78°F). The seed is very small, but try to sow as thinly as possible and do not cover with compost. Prick out when the seedlings have two sets of true leaves. As a precaution against damping off disease, water the trays of seedlings from below by standing in water just until

Ageratum 'Blue Mink' is a good colour

the surface of the growing medium becomes damp.

BRACHYCOME* (HA)

Brachycome iberidifolia, the Swan River Daisy, produces fragrant cineraria-like flowers of blue, pink, purple and white shades from June to September. Growing to a height of 23 cm (9 inches) it is useful for group planting in the border. Sow in March/May in open ground.

CALENDULA*
Marigold (HA)

This old English flower will thrive in any open position. It rewards the sower with a glorious summer show of orange and yellow shades for almost

31

no effort. The large double-daisy-type flowers look colourful and last well in water. Growing to 30-60 cm (1-2 ft) high, recommended varieties are 'Radio' – deep orange, 'Lemon Queen' – yellow and 'Fiesta Gitana' – a colourful mixture. Sow in open ground from March to May. If you want to change the plants in a bed, the prolific self-seeding of marigolds could create something of a 'weed problem'. Once allocated an area, self-sown seedlings will go on flowering satisfactorily.

CALLISTEPHUS*
Aster (HHA)

Callistephus chinensis is an annual belonging to the same family as the perennial Michaelmas daisy. Although it had been a great favourite over the years, the high incidence of aster wilt disease had become a deterrent to many gardeners. Relatively recent successes in the breeding of strains with an acceptable degree of wilt resistance has changed this situation. Asters flower according to the variety from July until the first frosts. Recommended varieties are 'Milady' – dwarf varieties in colours of rose, blue, white and mixed, 'Lilliput' – miniature pompon and 'Super sinensis' single. All are excellent for bedding out. There are several forms ranging from the tall, feathery-headed ostrich plume type to the chrysanthemum flowered ones, including those with incurving petals. There are also those with miniature pompom flowers and – probably the best of all for weather resistance and flower arranging – the single

sinensis strain. Height ranges from 20-60 cm (8-24 inches); tall ones are ideal for cutting.

Sow under glass in March/April and keep at 15-20°C (60-68°F) to germinate. Plant out in well drained soil in a sunny position. Watch out for curling leaves – a sign of aphid attack to which the young plants are particularly prone. It has a stunting effect and adversely affects flowering prospects.

CENTAUREA*
Cornflower (HA)

Centaurea cyanus is an easy annual for any well-drained, sunny site. The cornflower is a sturdy border and cut-flower plant, and may be either true cornflower blue or red, pink, purple or white. The taller varieties, growing up to 90 cm (3 ft) high, may need support. Sow seeds from March to May or in September where they are to flower the following year. Do not try to transplant.

Another species is *C. moschata* or Sweet sultan. Its powder-puff flowers of yellow, pink, purple and white are sweetly scented and good for cutting. It grows to a height of 60 cm (2 ft). Sow seed in April/May where it is intended to flower.

CHRYSANTHEMUM*
(HA)

Large groups of the single flowered chrysanthemum, *Chrysanthemum carinatum*, growing 75 cm (2 ft) tall will make impressive mid-border plantings and also supply long-lasting cut flowers. Colours include bronze, yellow, red, purple and white. Some varieties have zones of contrasting colour around the flower centre.

All do well in sunny positions, but make sure the soil never dries out around the plants' roots as this sometimes results in collapse. Seed should be sown in the open from March to May. Pinching out the leading shoot encourages branching and increases flower production. Seed mixtures are available.

CLARKIA* (HA)

This annual will do well in most soils, situated either in sun or partial shade. With its naturally branching habit it quickly covers the planting area and then flowers continuously from July to September. *Clarkia elegans* grows up to 60 cm (2 ft) high and produces long double flower spikes in shades of purple, red, pink and orange to white. *Clarkia pulchella* grows to 45 cm (18 inches) high and has double and semi-double flowers of white, violet and rose. Sow seed from March to May directly into the position where it is intended to flower.

COREOPSIS* (HA)

This will succeed in any well-drained soil – a light type being preferable – in a sunny position. It is a good choice in an industrial area because it will tolerate a polluted atmosphere. Depending on variety, plants reach 30-60 cm (1-2 ft) and produce daisy-like flowers continuously from July to September. Colours range from the more common yellow to crimson and scarlet. Those with petals contrastingly blotched towards the centre are particularly attractive. Sow seed mixtures in situ from March to May.

COSMOS* (HHA)

This is a tall-growing plant and very useful to bring colour to the back of the flower border. It has attractive finely cut foliage and bright dahlia-like flowers which are ideal for cutting. Cosmos will stand a dry season and is an ideal subject for a light, poor soil. Some support could be needed by flowering time which is in August and September.

Seed can be sown in a cool greenhouse, but I sow in situ in April/May. Although described as a half-hardy plant, shedded seed often survives the winter. It is certainly worth leaving self-sown seedlings; just thin them out and leave them to flower where they appear. Our choice is 'Sensation Mixed' which grows to 90 cm (3 ft).

DAHLIA**(HHA)

The bedding type of dahlia is usually grown as an annual. As such it has become one of the most valuable of the late summer flowerers. Blooms, in forms and colours similar to those of the larger border dahlias, appear in profusion from July going on until they are cut down by the first frosts. Dead-heading and cutting for decoration encourages the formation of more flowers. 'Chi Chi' and 'Redskin' are good colour mixtures.

For best results, a well-cultivated soil is necessary and the plants need watering well during dry spells. They grow only to a maximum height of 39 cm (15 inches) so no staking is needed.

Sow seed in the greenhouse at a temperature 15-20°C (60-68°F) in March and prick out,

putting eighteen seedlings in each standard sized tray. Plant out the small plants at the end of May/beginning of June after all danger of frost.

DELPHINIUM* (HA)

Larkspur, *Delphinium consolida*, is the annual delphinium, often grown especially for summer flower arrange-

The delicate mixed colours of Centaurea cyanus, the cornflower

ments. Its tall slender stems are covered with pink, blue or white flowers from June to August. The double sorts are particularly beautiful. 'Stock flowered' mixture is one of the best especially for cut flowers. It grows to 90 cm (3 ft).

33

Godetia has very beautiful flowers produced in great profusion

Seed may be sown in the open from March to May but if you want early flowers, sow in the previous September. The plants do best in a good moisture-retaining soil in full sun. Water them during dry spells.

DIANTHUS* (HHA)

Some of the newer varieties of the annual *Dianthus chinensis* are a must for a brilliant summer show. 'Heddewigii' has single flowers in scarlets, reds, pinks, mixtures and white, produced in succession from June until the first frosts. Other outstanding varieties are 'Queen of Hearts', which grows to 30 cm (12 inches) and has scarlet-red flowers and 'Snow Fire' which has white flowers with bright scarlet centres, and is a little smaller at 20 cm (8 inches). The bushy plants appreciate a neutral to alkaline soil in a position that gets plenty of sunshine. Sow under glass at a temperature of 15-20°C (60-68°F) in February/ March for planting out at the end of May.

DIMORPHOTHECA* (HA)

Dimorphotheca aurantiaca is a bright daisy-like flower from South Africa commonly known as 'Star of the Veldt'. It loves a dryish border, but do not plant it in shade as its flowers only open in bright light. I sow in the open from March to May where I intend it to flower. For a glorious display sow *D. aurantiaca* hybrids.

ECHIUM* (HA)

Echium plantagineum has a long flowering season. If sown early it will start to flower in late May and go on continuously until the autumn. The bees love its lovely bell-like flowers that come in shades of blue and pink. Most sites and soils are suitable but flowering is freer in full sun. Sow in the open where intended to flower from March to May. We sow 'Dwarf Hybrid' mixture, which grows to 30 cm (12 inches) high.

ESCHSCHOLZIA*

Californian Poppy (HA)

Grown as a hardy annual, *E. californica* produces masses of orange-yellow poppy flowers from June to October. 'Balerina' mixed is an interesting variety which has semi-double flowers with fluted petals.

The poppy does best in the poorer sandy soils and is just right for a dry sunny border. Self-sown seedlings will flower well in succeeding seasons. Sow in situ outdoors from March to May.

GAILLARDIA* (HHA)

Give *G. pulchella* a mid-border position where it will flower freely from July to October, providing, also, incidentally, a good flower for cutting. Try 'Suttons Large-flowered Mixed' which grows to 75 cm (2½ ft) or 'Goblin' (dwarf bedder), which is half the height at 38 cm (15 inches). Varieties with large flower heads will need support.

I sow seed in the greenhouse in March and keep at a temperature of 15°C (60°F) planting out at the end of May/beginning of June. The plants do well in sun or light shade in almost any soil although a well-drained soil is best.

GAZANIA**(HHA)

This is a half-hardy annual from South Africa that loves sunshine, in fact its brilliant daisy flowers close at night. Seed mixtures are available which give flowers of yellow, pink and red shades as well as the more usual orange.

I sow in the greenhouse heated to 15-20°C (60-68°F) in March for planting out at the end of May/beginning of June. It likes a well-drained sunny position.

GODETIA* (HA)

G. grandiflora is easy to grow and flowers prolifically in any soil. The plants are bushy and grow quickly, so they will soon cover the ground in the lower border. Clusters of poppy-type flowers are produced in profusion from June to August. Try 'Tall Double Mixed' which grows to 60 cm (2 ft) or 'Double Azalea-flowered Mixed' which grows to 35 cm (14 inches). I sow seed in an open sunny position in April where intended to flower, barely covering the seed.

HELIANTHUS* (HA)

There are many daisy-like flowers among the annuals but this plant – *H. annuus*, the sunflower – must be the most spectacular. From the tallest varieties, 3.2-4 metres (8-10 ft) stems topped by flowers measuring 30 cm (12 inches) across, are by no means unusual. These giants need lots of sun and a good, well-drained soil with plenty of water during dry spells. Support the stems with strong stakes. Shorter varieties are available, needing lighter support, and they will flower impressively in the centre of a bed or towards the back of the flower border but remember

The sunflower, Helianthus, is a most spectacular garden flower

HELIOTROPIUM* (HHA)

Many people know this as Cherry pie. Its sturdy naturally branching plants bear forget-me-not-like flowers from May to October. The dark green to almost purple foliage of some varieties makes a useful contrast both to its own flowers and to other foliage in the bed. 'Marine', which grows 38 cm (15 inches) high is an outstanding variety. Sow in the greenhouse at a temperature of 15-20°C (60-68°F) in February/March and plant out into any well-drained soil in a sunny position.

HELIPTERUM* (HHA)

This is often listed by seedsmen as *Acroclinium*. It has a delicate daisy flower well suited for planting in the summer flower border and for drying for winter decoration. Its flowers, which appear in July and August and again have strawy petals, are ideally suited for drying; this is done in the same way as Helichrysum. 'Sandfordii' is an attractive yellow variety, growing 30 cm (12 inches) high.

I sow seeds direct into their flowering position in April/May. Poorish soil and a sunny site produce the best flowers.

IBERIS* Candytuft (HA)

This pretty border plant, *I. umbellata*, bears many clusters of pink, white or purple flowers. Being so easy to grow makes it one of the best for a child's first packet of seed. The plant will thrive in most ordinary garden soils. If successional sowings are made from March to May where it is intended to flower, the flower

the heads will always turn to face the south. The flowering period is from late July to September, and recommended varieties are 'Giant Yellow' which grows 2 metres (6 ft) high and 'Sunburst', which has mixed colours and grows to 1.2 metres (4 ft) tall. Sow in the flowering positions in April/May.

HELICHRYSUM* (HA)

The Strawflower, *H. bracteatum*, is certainly attractive in the garden as a bedding plant but its great value is to the flower arranger for drying. Again, the flowers are daisy-like in shape but the petals are shiny and somewhat like

The sweet pea, Lathyrus odoratus

straw. Flowers are produced from July to September and blooms for drying should be cut just as they are opening. If they are cut when fully open, seed development continues and the flower centres are spoilt. Try growing 'Hot Bikini' – a bright red and 'Bright Bikini' – a colourful mixture, both of which grow to 30 cm (12 inches) high. To dry remove all foliage from the stems and then hang them, flower heads downwards in small bunches in a shady cool airy place. Sow seed in March/May in open ground. A sandy soil in full sun is best.

ing season can extend from June to September. 'Giant Hyacinth' – a white and 'Red Flash' – a vivid carmine red are both successful varieties.

IMPATIENS**
Busy Lizzie (HHA)

The Busy Lizzie, *I. sultanii*, is perhaps more often thought of as a pot plant than a bedding subject. However when used for bedding brilliant splashes of colour and a complete ground cover can result, with continuous flowering from June to October. The tender horizontally growing stems which are so vulnerable when pot grown spread out quite safely over the surface of the garden soil. Impatiens will grow in any ordinary soil in sun or light shade provided it is never short of moisture. Try 'Futura' mixed.

Sow seeds in March/April under glass and keep at a temperature of 15-20°C (60-78°F). We use equal parts of peat and sand seed compost mixture and do not cover the seed. Never let the compost dry out after germination.

LATHYRUS*
Sweet Pea (HA)

The sweet pea, *L. odoratus*, is a great favourite. From June to September the lovely flowers in shades of red, pink, salmon, blue, lavender and white are a delight in the garden and for indoor flower arrangements. The tall 'Spencer' varieties all need sticks or some form of support as does 'Jet Set' mixed which grows 90 cm (3 ft) tall. 'Snoopea' mixed 30-38 cm (12-15 inches) tall and needs no support, making it excellent for a border. As for all mem-

bers of the pea family, an alkaline soil is required. Sow seed in January to March under glass at a temperature of 15-20°C (60-68°F) or in April/May in open ground.

LAVATERA* (HA)

The Annual Mallow, *L. trimestris*, is an erect plant, which grows to around 75 cm (2½ ft) tall, branches naturally and is a good space filler. The wide petals of its pink or white flowers form a beautiful open trumpet up to 10 cm (4 inches) across and appear from July to September. Recommended varieties are 'Silver Cup' which grows 60 cm (2 ft) tall

The annual mallow, Lavatera trimestris

and 'Mont Blanc' which is white and a little shorter at 50 cm (20 inches) tall. Sunny sites on ordinary soils are suitable. Sow the seed in situ in April.

LIMONIUM*
Statice, Sea Lavender (HHA)

The sprays of small yellow, pink, lavender, blue and white flowers decorate this plant from July to September. They are excellent for drying if you cut them just as they begin to open. 'Rainbow' mixture is a recommended variety: it grows 45 cm (18 inches) tall. Any ordinary soil is suitable for this plant. I sow seed from January to March under glass at a temperature of 15-20°C (60-68°F) for planting out at the end of May.

LOBELIA* (HHA)

The compact form of this plant which grows about 10 cm (4 inches) high makes it ideal as an edging plant. The trailing varieties are excellent for containers and hanging baskets. Recommended varieties are 'Cambridge Blue' – a sky blue, and 'Crystal Palace' – a deep blue, while 'Blue Cascade Pendula' is the one for hanging baskets. To enjoy a long period of flowering the plants should not dry out.

I sow seed in the greenhouse at a temperature of 18-20°C (65-68°F) from January to March and prick out in tiny clumps of four or five to plant out at the end of May.

MALCOMIA*
Virginian Stock (HA)

The low growing drifts of small rose, lilac and white sweet-scented flowers of *M. maritima* appear very quickly after sowing the seeds of this plant. For a continuous show, make successional sowings of mixed seed from March to May in a sunny position where you want it to flower.

MATTHIOLA*
Night-scented Stock (HA)

This well-known plant, *M. bicornis*, is not much to look at during the day but at night it opens its pale lilac flowers and gives out a sweet heavy scent. It is especially fragrant on a still warm evening. Sow seed from March to May where you want it to flower in any garden soil in sun or partial shade.

MESEMBRYAN-THEMUM** (HHA)

The Livingstone Daisy is a sun-loving, succulent-leaved native of South Africa which spreads brilliance over the driest of sunny sites. Masses of bright red, pink, orange, yellow and white daisy flowers appear continuously from June to August. A position in full sun is essential as the flowers only open when it shines. Try growing 'Sparkler', which grows to 10 cm (4 inches).

I sow seed in the greenhouse at 18-20°C (65-68°F) in February/March for planting out at the end of May.

MIMULUS** (HHA)

The native growing area of mimulus, the Monkey Flower, is boggy so it is well suited to planting in damp places and light shade. Flowers mainly in shades of gold or blotched mahogany are produced freely from June to September. After the initial flowering, pinch back the leading shoots to encourage branching and ensure continuous flowering.

I sow in the greenhouse at a temperature of 15-20°C (60-68°F) in February/March for planting out at the end of May into as moisture-retentive a soil as possible.

MOLUCCELLA**
Bells of Ireland (HHA)

The tall flower spikes of *M. laevis* reach up to 90 cm (3 ft) and consist of tiny white flowers, each surrounded by a light green shell-like calyx. They are highly valued by flower arrangers for drying and cut flower use. The plant will survive in any garden soil in an open sunny position, but dryish conditions seem to give the best results. Sow seeds under glass in March at 15°C (60°F) to plant out at the end of May.

NEMESIA* (HHA)

This is an early flowering annual which puts on a show from the end of May to August. Growing to a height of 20-30 cm (8-12 inches) it is a good subject for beds and borders. 'Carnival Mixed' produces compact plants of glorious colours. Keep the soil moist if the plants are to flower well for a long time.

I sow under glass in March at a temperature of 15-20°C (60-68°F) for planting out at the end of May. Do not allow to stand in the tray any longer than need be. Tray-bound plants do not become bushy in the way they should.

NEMOPHILA*
Baby Blue Eyes (HHA)

This annual, *N. insignis*, has a useful spreading habit and from June to August it forms a carpet of bright blue, white-centred saucer-shaped flowers. It may be grown in sun or partial shade, but it likes a good moisture-retentive soil. Sow in March in the open where you want it to flower.

NICOTIANA*
Tobacco Plant (HHA)

Beautiful trumpet-shaped flowers borne from late June to September and generally very fragrant are the feature of this plant. Older varieties open in the evening only, and while newer varieties do open during the daytime as well, the breeding in of day-long opening seems to have resulted in the loss of scent. Blooms stand up to rain well, although the taller varieties growing up to 90 cm (3 ft) need some support. The newer, free flowering dwarf varieties do

Nemesia with its rich colours

not need support. Choose from 'Evening Fragrance' – mixed colours growing 90 cm (3 ft) tall, 'Crimson Rock', growing 45 cm (18 inches) tall and 'Lime Green' growing to 75 cm (2½ ft) tall.

Sow seeds under glass in March at 15-18°C (60-65°F) for planting out in late May.

PAPAVER* Poppies (HA)

Tall stems support the cupped yellow, red, orange and white heads of these flowers as they sway in the breeze from June to August. Recommended varieties are 'Shirley Poppy' which produces single or double flowers and grows 60 cm (2 ft) high and 'Paeony-flowered' Mixed which grows to 90 cm (3 ft) high. I sow seed in April in good ordinary soil in full sun.

PETUNIA* (HHA)

Petunias, with their trumpet-shaped flowers, are available in many colours, some with white edgings or star markings and bicolours. Some of the newer varieties are earlier, freer flowering and more weather resistant than their predecessors. Try 'Resisto Rose' and 'Red Joy' plus other colours in the same series.

Sow under glass in early March at a temperature of 15-20°C (60-68°F) for planting out at the end of May. To ensure good plants, the seedlings should never receive a check at any time. Prick out before they become drawn. Plant in any good garden soil preferably after it has been well cultivated to allow an easy root run, thus enabling the plants to take up all the moisture they need. Water well between the plants during dry spells.

PHACELIA* (HA)

P. campanularia is a small bushy plant, growing only 23 cm (9 inches) high; flowers from June to September. The flowers are deep blue and bell-shaped and the foliage gives off a fragrance when pinched. This plant does best in a light well-drained soil and is well suited for small informal sowings towards the front of the flower border. I make successive sowings from March to June where I want it to flower.

PHLOX* (HHA)

Phlox drummondii is an easily maintained bedding plant which is equally suitable for container planting. Dense heads of yellow, red, pink, purple, lavender and white flowers from July to September. Sow under glass in March at 15°C (60°F) for planting out at the end of May.

PORTULACA** (HHA)

This is a somewhat neglected annual which deserves wider use. It is a neat plant with succulent foliage that enables it to withstand a degree of drought. It can really only be said to grow 15 cm (6 inches) tall as the stems tend to lie along the ground. Semi-double flowers with prettily ruffled petals in shades of most colours (except blue) appear successively from June to September. The flowers wait for sunlight before opening fully and then form a complete carpet of colour and decorative foliage. Recommended varieties are *P. grandiflora* 'Double Mixed' or F_2 and 'Calypso'.

Sow under glass in March at a temperature of 18°C (65°F), and never overhead water the seedlings – instead water from below by placing the trays of seedlings in water. Plant out at the end of May in a sunny position in any ordinary soil.

SALPIGLOSSIS** (HHA)

This plant is so beautiful and exotic to look at that it gives the impression it is harder to grow than it really is! Trumpet-shaped flowers, some attractively veined, are carried on slender stems and open in succession from July to September. At a height of 45-60 cm (18-24 inches) it is a striking mid-border plant; try growing F_1 'Splash'. Water in dry weather to maintain flowering. Sow seed under glass in February at 18°C (65°C) to plant out at the end of May.

SALVIA* (HA and HHA)

Salvia horminum (HA) is an unusual bushy plant which produces brightly coloured terminal bracts of blue, pink, purple or white. These are the plant's real attraction as they outshine the much smaller flowers. The plant makes a striking addition to the flower border. Sow under glass in March at a temperature of 15-18°C (60-65°F) for planting out at the end of May.

Salvia Splendens (HHA), although not one of the easiest of subjects to grow, still remains a firm favourite. The flower spikes – usually red or scarlet – are always brilliant and appear from July until the first frosts. Recommended varieties are 'Carabiniere' – scarlet-red, growing 38 cm (15 inches) tall and 'Volcano' – an intense bright red, which grows to the same height. Keep a watch out for slugs. Sow seed under glass in February at 15-18°C (60-68°F) for planting out in late May.

TAGETES* Marigold (HHA)

In its various forms all of which are easy to grow, this is a most accommodating annual. *Tagetes erecta*, the African marigold is the tallest and largest flowered. It begins its flowering a little later than the smaller types as big plants take longer to mature. However the show provided by the large lemon-yellow to bright orange blooms from June until the first frosts is always splendid. Try 'Gay Ladies' mixed which grows 45 cm (18 inches) tall. *T. patula*, French marigolds, are compact, bushy and very free flowering. They flower from late May until the first frosts and can completely clothe the planting area with masses of individual, long-

lasting blooms. There are singles, doubles and variants in plenty; try 'Queen Sophia', which is an outstanding double. Amongst the new Afro-French marigolds 'Suzie Wong', 'Moll Flanders' and 'Nell Gwyn' are all excellent, and grow to a height of 30 cm (12 inches). *Tagetes tenuifolia pumila* is the plant commonly known as tagetes. Small bushy plants with finely cut foliage are covered with small single gold, lemon or mahogany daisy-like flowers from July to September. It is a particularly good edging plant; try 'Golden Gem'.

Tagetes as a group require very little heat for germination. I sow all types in the greenhouse in March at a temperature of 15°C (60°F) for planting out at the end of May.

TROPAEOLUM*
Nasturtium (HA)

Do not dismiss the nasturtium, *T. majus*, as being too ordinary; trailing varieties cover banks, fences or any 'eyesore' with cheerful, colourful efficiency from June to September with minimum demands on soil or gardening skill. The dwarf varieties will grow happily in any sunny spot in need of colour. Try 'Gleam' hybrids, which have double flowers and grow 38 cm (15 inches) tall and 'Mixed tall single' a climbing variety which grows up to 1.8 metres (6 ft). Sow in situ, April to May.

VERBENA* (HHA)

The heads of primrose-like flowers in shades of red, pink, blue and white, often faintly scented, are borne in profusion by these sturdy little plants from June until the first frosts. Outstanding varieties are 'Derby Salmon Rose' and 'Derby Scarlet'. Sow seed under glass in February at temperatures of 15-20°C (60-68°F) for planting out at the end of May.

XERANTHEMUM* (HA)

X. annuum is one of the best plants to grow for the production of everlasting flowers. Growing to a height of 60 cm (2 ft), the strawy-petalled white, pink, lilac or purple daisy-like flowers keep their true colours for years if cutting and drying are carried out properly (see under *Helichrysum bracteatum*,

page 36). Sow March to April where you want them to flower, in a good light soil.

ZEA*
Ornamental Maize (HHA)

This plant, *Zea mays japonica*, produces an ornamental corn cob which can be cut when fully ripe for drying and winter decoration. Try 'Strawberry Corn' which grows to 60 cm (3 ft).

Sow under glass in March at a temperature of 15-20°C (60-68°F). Plant out at the end of May in a sunny spot and fertile soil, putting plants in a square block to assist pollination and the formation of seed.

ZINNIA** (HHA)

Z. elegans is a bright, sun-loving annual which flowers from July to September. Some varieties are quite tall, growing up to 90 cm (3 ft), but the strong stems and firm flower heads are excellent for cutting. Try 'Ruffles Mixture' or select separate colours; they grow 60 cm (2 ft) high.

Sow in the greenhouse in March at a temperature of 15-18°C (60-68°F) for planting out at the end of May. If possible, plant into a rich well cultivated soil in a sunny but sheltered position.

The marigold, Tagetes

BIENNIALS

All the plants in this list will flower properly in the season following that when the seed was sown. However it is important to sow the seeds during the period recommended on the seed packet as the length of daylight determines when and how the flowering will occur. Seed of biennials sown too early may produce flowers of very poor quality towards the end of that season instead of their best blooms as nature intends the year after the seed germinates.

ALTHAEA* Hollyhocks

Whilst hollyhocks can be grown as annuals or perennials it is more usual nowadays to treat them as biennials. By doing so it is possible to minimise the risk of hollyhock rust, a disease which becomes a scourge on old plants especially in the warmer and dryer parts of the country.

Sow the seed outdoors in May or June in a well prepared seed bed. Space out the strongest seedlings so as to get strong plants for planting out in late summer. Hollyhocks do best in dry, sunny positions especially when they have the protection of a wall or fence; that is why I always associate them with cottage gardens.

Both the double and the single varieties come true to colour from seed. If you enjoy watching bees at work, grow Sutton's 'Single Brilliant-Mixture'; the bees simply love the wide open flowers. For double flowers, Chater's 'Double Mixed' is an excellent selection. 'Summer Carnival' also produces a good mixture of fully double flowers which grow low down the stems.

BELLIS* Daisy

The common species, *Bellis perennis*, is the well-known, un-loved lawn weed, but there are various large-flowered and double minia-ture varieties well worth considering giving space in the flower garden. For example *Bellis perennis* 'Monstrosa' with its double flowers that reach 5 cm (2 inches) or more across and have a colour range from white through pink to scarlet red, makes an excellent bedding plant. It is at its best in May/June, and is sometimes catalogued as 'Goliath Mixed'. Among the miniature varieties are 'Pomponette' which has tightly quilled double daisies in shades of red, rose and white; 'Lilliput' which has crimson flowers; 'Dresden China' which has pink; 'Red Buttons' – carmine-red, and 'Rob Roy' – red. The advantage of growing 'Dresden China' and 'Rob Roy' is that neither produces seeds to cause an unwanted plant-weed problem. Instead they have to be propagated by division of parent plants, so are available from nurseries as bedding plants.

Sow the seeds of other varieties outside in June in shallow drills in a seed bed. Transplant them to their permanent quarters in September.

CAMPANULA MEDIUM* Canterbury Bell

These are the traditional Canterbury Bells, which with their 'cups and saucers' are still great favourites in cottage gardens. I feel that they merit a place, if only a small one, in any flower garden. Special seed mixtures are available of 'Calycanthema', which grows up to 75-90 cm (2½-3 ft) high and has softly coloured flowers in white, rose and various shades of blue. Dwarf Bedding Mixture seed is available for plants that only grow 45 cm (18 inches) high, but the flowers, although produced in a similar colour range, have single blooms without 'saucers'. However we have grown one of these mixtures, namely 'Bells of Holland', and found the dome-shaped plants looked attractive when bedded out in a border.

Sow the seed in May/June outdoors, thinly in shallow drills in a seedbed. Transplant in September.

CHEIRANTHUS* Wallflower

Wallflowers, *Cheiranthus cheiri*, are particularly popular as late spring and early summer flowering bedding plants. They need to be well grown and established as bushy plants to stand the winter if they are to make a really good colourful and fragrant show in the spring. Being members of the brassica family they appreciate a soil with some calcium in it; it is necessary to add

garden lime to acid soils. This not only helps to grow good plants, but it also helps to prevent the disease club root attacking them.

For best results sow the seed in May/June, thinly in shallow drills in a seed bed. When the seedlings are large enough to handle, transplant them into rows 15-20 cm (6-8 inches) apart. At the same time, in order to ensure bushy plants pinch out the tips of the growing points. In October lift the plants and plant them where you want them to flower, bearing in mind they prefer a sunny position. The ground should have been well dug over and prepared, and limed if necessary.

There are numerous varieties to choose from; most of them make plants that grow 35-45 cm (15-18 inches) tall and which should be spaced about 30 cm (12 inches) apart. Our favourite single colour varieties are 'Fire King' – a brilliant scarlet; 'Blood Red' – with a colour that is true to its name; 'Vulcan' – a deep crimson and 'Cloth of Gold' – a yellow variety. For really startling displays in many colours plus plenty of fragrance, try either 'Persian Carpet' or 'Colour Cascade'. These mixtures always look superb in small gardens.

Seed of dwarf varieties that grow about 22 cm (9 inches) high in the usual range of colours is available and these, of course, can be planted a little closer together.

The Siberian Wallflowers, C. × allionii, which grow about 30 cm (12 inches) high and have brilliant orange spikes of flowers, can also be planted slightly closer together than the tall wallflowers. The pro-

The popular Sweet William, Dianthus barbatus

cedure for growing them from seed is the same as for ordinary wallflowers.

DIANTHUS BARBATUS*
Sweet William
In recent years Sweet Williams have been greatly improved – some of the new varieties have really brilliant combinations of colour in massive clusters of flowers and there are some excellent varieties in single colours, too. Whichever type you grow, sow the seed outdoors in May/June in shallow drills in a seed bed, and transplant them into their flowering positions in October. Plant them 20-25 cm (8-10 inches) apart in bold blocks for the best effect. To do well they need a well-drained soil, a sunny position and if the soil is inclined to be

43

acid, a little garden lime added when preparing the bed.

The tall varieties grow up to 45 cm (18 inches) high and good ones to chose are 'Giant Auricula Eyed Mixed', 'Pink Beauty Improved', 'Scarlet Beauty' and 'Messenger Mixed'. A hybrid known as 'Sweet Wivelsfield' has large clusters of flowers in many colours. Among the dwarf varieties, which grow up to 25 cm (10 inches), 'Indian Carpet' in a glorious mixture of colours is outstanding.

DIGITALIS* Foxglove

Once introduced into your garden and allowed to seed you will soon have legions of seedlings every spring. If these are thinned out, they will make grand plants for flowering the following season. Whilst our native *Digitalis purpurea* is beautiful and interesting when seen growing wild in a woodland setting, it is wise to start in a garden with a packet of 'Excelsior' strain seed. From this you will get plants that are some 1.5 metres (5 ft) tall, with large spikes of flowers. Their joy is that they come in a far greater range of colours – white, cream or pink to purple – all with delightfully spotted throats. The more recently introduced 'Foxy' strain is similar but not so tall; it does well in partial shade where the soil does not dry out even in high summer.

May or June is the time to sow the very fine foxglove seed. Broadcast it over a well-prepared seed bed and lightly rake over the soil to cover the seed. When the seedlings are large enough to handle, space them out so they are 15 cm (6

inches) apart. Plant them out in September.

LUNARIA* Honesty

Lunaria annua is a must for the flower arranger's garden, and the real interest will be in the stems of silvery seed pods produced at the end of the summer. These are always in great demand for dried winter floral arrangements. Whilst the variety with purple flowers is generally the most popular, there are others which have white or pink flowers. The colour of the flowers, incidentally, make no significant differ-

The bright, purple flowers of honesty, Lunaria annua

ence to the quality of the seed pods. You will only need to sow honesty once if you allow the seed to shed; in fact seedling production is so prolific that it can become a weed.

To make a start sow the seed outside in May/June where you want it to flower. Thin out to 30 cm (12 inches) apart.

MYOSOTIS*

Forget-Me-Not

The ever popular Forget-me-not, *M. alpestris*, is a native

flower of Great Britain which, in the hands of the plant breeders, has been greatly improved for decorating our gardens. Even when grown without the company of other plants, the dainty flowers carried on thin stems are a delight in April and May. When seen flowering amongst a bed of tulips in full flower they make a sight never to be forgotten. There are varieties in colours other than blue, such as 'Carmine Red' and 'Victoria White', but for me a Forget-me-not must be blue. 'Royal Blue' which has rich dark blue flowers and grows 30 cm (12 inches) tall, is an excellent choice and there is a dwarf form of the same variety. It grows only 18 cm (7 inches) tall and has a more bushy growth habit. Plants will seed freely after flowering to produce plenty of seedlings.

To make a start, sow the seed in April or May outside in a seed bed for transplanting in September. The alternative is simply to sow the seed in the flowering position and thin out the seedlings. A site in full sun or partial shade is ideal.

VIOLA* Pansy

This group of flowers includes both the viola and the garden pansy (*V.* × *wittrockiana*) which is still the most popular. A vast number of varieties are available but for me, it is the flowers with 'pansy faces' that have the greatest appeal; in fact I started my gardening at the age of six with a penny packet of pansy seed and I still love to see them smiling in the sunshine.

The superb strain of Swiss giant pansies called 'Roggli Giant' Mixed is well known and a packet of seed will have many colours. 'Tiara' Mixed, which has large flowers is a good variety as are 'Engelmann's Giants'. The lighter coloured faces of 'Love Duet' Mixed are simply charming. Amongst the faceless pansies, 'Azure Blue', which is a clear blue with a yellow eye, is excellent and 'Golden Champion' and 'Clear Crystal' Mixed also deserve a mention. However, these are only a few of the many good varieties.

Violas make compact plants with somewhat smaller flowers freely produced throughout the spring and summer in the most surprising colour combinations.

Viola, the smiling garden pansy

After the first flush of flowering of pansies it is wise to cut back the plants, spray them for aphids and give them a feed. Then you will be able to enjoy another longer flowering period. The best time to sow the seed of both pansies and violas is in June/July outside in shallow drills. Prick out the seedlings as soon as they are large enough to handle so they have room to grow into showy plants. Then transplant into their flowering positions in September/October. Propagation by soft cuttings taken in June or July is possible but they will need shading until rooted. This is a certain way of building up a stock of a pansy or viola of which you are particularly fond and do not wish to lose.

HARDY PERENNIALS

These are plants which once established in a border will go on growing and flowering for several seasons. Whilst most can be grown from seed it is usually better to start with young plants of named varieties. Before planting always make sure that the planting sites are free from perennial weed roots, otherwise an uncontrollable weed problem will develop.

ACHILLEA*

All varieties are members of the yarrow family, and they have aromatic fern-like foliage and round heads of clusters of small closely packed flowers. The plants do best in dry, sunny situations and they should be divided and replanted in the spring. If they are left undisturbed for several seasons, the flowers deteriorate.

The following are good varieties for the herbaceous border: 'Coronation Gold', which flowers in July/August, bearing golden yellow heads on slender stems clothed in silver grey foliage and grows 90 cm (3 ft) tall; 'Gold Plate' – a taller variety that can grow up to 1.2 metres (4 ft) tall and flowers from July through to September, bearing large golden yellow flowers heads on stiff stems clothed in grey-green foliage, and 'Moonshine' – a dwarf variety growing only 60 cm (2 ft) high and very useful for the front of the border. This is a new pale yellow hybrid with silver foliage. This is the variety to choose for the flower arranger's garden.

ALCHEMILLA*

Lady's Mantle

This well-loved plant, A. mollis, produces its clouds of tiny lime-green flowers in June. However, it is its pale green foliage that makes it so truly lovely. It is most useful for the flower arranger and has been recommended as a ground cover plant but I have not tried growing it this way. It is easily grown from seed, sown outside in spring, or by division in the spring, and will thence forward seed itself freely.

ALSTROEMERIA*

The Peruvian Lily, A. amaryllidaceae, is a species that varies considerably in hardiness, so to be on the safe side, plant the fleshy roots at least 15 cm (6 inches) deep. It is a good plan to raise your own plants from seed which should be very fresh or foil-packed. Sow very thinly in trays or pots in spring, and put these in a cool greenhouse. Germination time will vary greatly in relation to the freshness of the seed; it can be a month – it can be six months. When the seedlings are large enough to handle put them individually into 8 cm (3½ inch) pots, trying to disturb the roots as little as possible. When they are well established plant them outside about 30 cm (12 inches) apart in the warmest sheltered position possible, again with the minimum of root disturbance. They are happiest when the soil is deep, on the dry side with some sand in it and drains well.

One of the hardiest varieties is 'Aurantiaca' which grows to 90 cm (3 ft); its 4 cm (1½ inch) orange flowers are streaked red. The 'Ligtu' hybrids, which grow 60 cm (2 ft) tall, and are well known for their pale pink, pale lilac or whitish trumpet shaped flowers are also a good choice. Both flower from June to August and will provide excellent cut flower material.

ALYSSUM*

The commonly grown plant, A. saxatile, has grey foliage and light yellow clusters of flowers that appear in profusion in the spring. It grows to a height of about 30 cm (12 inches). Whilst it is not fussy about the soil, it does prefer to have as much of the sunshine as possible. The stems are lanky and unless the plants are cut back after flowering they soon become untidy looking. It is very easily propagated from cuttings taken after flowering.

ANCHUSA*

Anchusa azurea is listed as a perennial but with us it is a rather short-life plant so I treat it as a biennial. It does prefer somewhat drier and sunnier situations than we have. We grow our plants from seed sown outdoors in May/June in a seed bed. After a couple of months they are thinned and we plant them out in their flowering positions in October. If you grow them from rooted off-sets, do not take these until the spring otherwise you will have winter losses. If you prefer to buy plants, April is the best time. 'Loddon Royalist' is a splendid, relatively new variety. Although it grows 90 cm (3 ft) tall, it has a bushy habit and should not require staking to keep its large royal blue flowers off the ground. 'Morning Glory', which grows to 1.2 metres (4 ft), has super gentian-blue flowers on tall stems which will need support. 'Royal Blue' also has pure gentian-blue flowers which, like other varieties, appear in June. It grows 90 – 120 cm (3-4 ft) high and needs staking, otherwise the plants will be untidy and you will lose much of their beauty. Even taller, growing to 1.2 – 1.5 metres (4 ft) is 'Azurea Dropmore', which has rich deep blue flowers that appear just a little bit later on in the summer.

AQUILEGIA* Columbine

Our native *Aquilegia vulgaris*, so charmingly known as Granny's Bonnet, has mainly blue or purple flowers with short spurs and is indeed inferior to some of the hybrids now available. Aquilegia seeds freely and we have found it necessary to ruthlessly eliminate seedlings from blue and purple flowers, otherwise these colours become dominant in the self-sown areas. Aquilegias appreciate some light shade in a situation where the soil is likely to be moist and cool. Ours grow happily in a shrub border.

The long-spurred hybrids are most attractive with their many combinations of col-

The graceful and dainty aquilegia with its delicate flowers

ours, from crimson through to the delicate shades of pink, yellows and white. The 'McKana Giant Hybrids' which grow 75-90 cm (2½ – 3 ft) tall are outstanding, and can be grown from seed sown outside or from plants purchased in the spring.

We have also grown *A. alpina* with its pretty blue and

white flowers, but it does not always come true to colour when grown from seed. It grows 30 cm (12 inches) tall. We also have a great affection for *A. formosa* with its dainty brick-red flowers produced on slender stems. Growing to 90 cm (3 ft), it is so graceful and as a bonus it will come true from seed.

Do remember that greenfly unfortunately will simply adore your aquilegias.

ARABIS* Rock Cress
These trailing plants that grow no more than 15 cm (6 inches) high are especially suitable for rockeries and walls. Flowering commences early in the spring when it is a beautiful sight, but unfortunately it does not last very long. The plants are easily grown in ordinary soil; all they need is good drainage and tidying up after flowering.

Grown from seed sown either in a cold frame in March/April or outside in May/June. Seed in the separate colours – white, pink or rose-purple – is catalogued, as well as mixtures of the colours. All will give you mass displays of their tiny flowers.

ARMERIA* Thrift
Our native sea pink *Armeria maritima* will be found growing wild along much of our

The tiny flowers of rock cress, Arabis

Western coastline, where, in late spring and early summer, its masses of pink or pinkish-lilac rounded flower-heads borne on short stems produce beauty on a grand scale. We have found a place for a few plants we brought back from the west coast of Scotland, but it is 'Giant Pink' with its 45-60 cm (18-24 inches) stems which we grew from seeds, that gives us a great show without a break from early spring to autumn. Sow the seed in March/April outside in a seed bed to flower the following season.

'Vindictive' is an improved form of *A. maritima* which has rich rose-crimson rounded flowerheads. Early spring would be the time to order plants of named varieties.

ASTER* Michaelmas Daisy
If Michaelmas daisies, *A. novi-belgii*, are perhaps not quite as popular as they were some years ago, the decline could be traced to mildew. Happily, however, this can now be minimised by giving the plants a good start. It is old, over-crowded plants grown in dry soils, especially in the shade of trees, which suffer most from mildew. Michaelmas daisies will really thrive, flower well and have healthy growth if divided and re-planted each March in a well-prepared rich moist soil. Putting bonemeal in the planting hole and watering early in any drought period will help greatly. As with so many diseases, it is the growing conditions and the weather that determine whether or not mildew is going to be a problem. If the weather is very dry, a timely spray with a fungicide may give control.

For autumn border displays, Michaelmas daisies are without equal, blooming first in September and going on right through October. As this is a time when autumn gales often occur, it is advisable to provide some support. A few twiggy sticks put around the plants early in the growing season is an answer without being unsightly.

There are many good named varieties with heights ranging from 60-120 cm (2-4 ft in colours from crimson-red through to light pink and blue. A few I know well are: 'Ada Ballard' – which has lavender blue flowers and grows 90 cm (3 ft) tall; 'Crimson Brocade' which has semi-double, rose crimson flowers and grow

48

90 cm (3 ft) tall; 'Ernest Ballard', which has very large semi-double rose crimson flowers and grows 90 cm (3 ft) tall, and 'Pride of Colwall', which has double violet-blue flowers and grows 75 cm (2½ ft) tall. New plants should be purchased from the nursery in March and planted straightaway for flowering the same year.

ASTILBE* False Goat's Beard
An easy-to-grow perennial provided there is plenty of moisture in the soil at all times of the year. The colourful plumes produced during the summer are most attractive. They are at their best in partial shade. Available in colours from white through pinks and lilacs to deepest red, good varieties included 'Bressingham Beauty' – rich pink; 'Deutschland' – intense white; 'Fanal' – deep red. Planting time: October – March. Prop-

agation is by division of the roots, March/April. For maximum flowering lift and divide the plants every third year.

AUBRIETA*
This low-growing plant is well known for its mass displays early in the spring. Ideal for dry sunny positions, plant it in a rock garden or in pockets in a dry wall and it will soon spread itself out into large mat-like plants. Do not be tempted to despise it because it is common; if you plant named varieties or grow your plants from seed, you can have a considerable range of colours.

Sow seeds in March in trays and put in the greenhouse. When the seedlings are large enough to handle prick them out into pots. They will be ready for planting in their final positions in October.

Of the named varieties, I can recommend the following: 'Barker's Double' – deep rosy

purple, 'Bressingham Pink', 'Dr. Mules' – violet purple, and 'Riverslea' – mauve pink. Do not be afraid to cut aubrietas back immediately after flowering; they will benefit.

BERGENIA*
These are plants of the saxifrage family and are excellent subjects for planting in dry borders, amongst shrubs or even conifers, as they are able to flourish in deep shade. They should certainly find a place in every flower arranger's garden. In March and April, the branching sprays of close set flowers produced on short fleshy stems are at their best. For the rest of the year, the foliage also has its value. In spring the young bold evergreen foliage is a green colour, but as it ages it takes on most attractive hues of red and

A clump of sea pink, Armeria maritima

bronze. The most popular species is *B. cordifolia*, which grows 45 cm (18 inches) high and finds favour as a plant for the border and for cutting for flower arrangements. Its pink flower heads are carried on long stems. *B. cordifolia purpurea* has the same growing habit but its flowers are a deeper rose-crimson. The lower growing *B. delavayi* is also popular. It grows to 30 cm (12 inches) high and has evergreen, crimson-backed foliage which turns dark, bronzy purple in the winter. Propagation is by division of plants in the spring. Plants can be grown from seed sown in the greenhouse but germination is rather unpredictable.

CAMPANULA* Bellflower

Within this group, there is great variety ranging from dwarf alpines to large herbaceous plants. None is particularly fussy about growing conditions but do best in cool, rich limestone soils where there are good moisture levels combined with adequate drainage. It is impossible to list more than a few, all of which make excellent subjects for the herbaceous border and which flower in June/July. They are: *C. glomerata dahurica*, which has violet-purple flowers and grows 45 cm (18 inches) tall; *C. lactiflora* 'Loddon Anna', which has lilac-pink flowers and grows 75 cm (2½ ft) tall; *C. lactiflora* 'Pritchard's Variety', which has pale violet-blue flowers and grows 90 cm (3 ft) tall; and *C. macrantha* which has foxglove-like spikes of amethyst-violet flowers and grows 105 cm (3½ ft) tall. At the other end of the scale,

there is *C. lactiflora* 'Pouffe', which at 23 cm (9 inches) is a real dwarf. It has lavender-blue starlike flowers, and along with some many others, is well worth considering.

Campanulas are easily propagated by division of the roots in the spring and that is also the time to plant new acquisitions from a nursery. If growing from seed, sow early in spring in seed compost, and protect the trays from the weather in either a cold frame or cold greenhouse. Plant out in their flowering positions in May/June.

CATANANCHE*
Cupid's Dart

A very suitable plant for the border, *C. caerulea* grows some 60 cm (2 ft) tall and has starlike purple-blue flowers that are not unlike cornflowers but with darker eyes. It is one of those 'cut-and-come again' plants and it will flower almost continuously from July till September if cut back after flowering. However, it does sometimes suffer from a desire to produce too many flowers at the end of the season, so reduce the number of flower buds in September to keep the plant in good condition for the following season. Anyone interested in flower arranging will find it very useful, not only as a summer flower but also for preserving.

It does well on light soils in sunny positions where the drainage is good, and it resents wet winter soil conditions. It is easy to propagate from root cuttings taken in the autumn or from spring-sown seed kept in a cold greenhouse to germinate.

CERASTIUM*
Snow in Summer

Cerastium tomentosum is a mat-forming plant, that grows only 15 cm (6 inches) high. It has lovely grey foliage which is covered with small white flowers in May and June. Very suitable for dry walls and sunny positions that need covering, it is really less suitable for the rockery as it is too invasive. It is easily grown from seed sown outside in April/May, either straight in its flowering position or in a seed bed.

CHRYSANTHEMUM*

For the herbaceous border, spray varieties of this popular flower are best. These require little attention during the growing season except for some support to prevent wind damage at flowering time. Keep a watchful eye open for greenfly and possible mildew signs and take appropriate action to prevent either of these causing damage (see p.17). All chrysanthemums appreciate well prepared soils with good drainage in open situations.

We have derived enormous pleasure from growing the following garden varieties which all have double flowers: 'Pennine Bright Eyes' – pink, 'Pennine Crimson', 'Pennine Orange', 'Pennine Yellow' and 'Pennine White', as well as some of the single spray varieties such as 'Pennine Dream' – pink, 'Pennine Globe' – gold, and 'Pennine Tango' – a bronze. Most of these grow 90-120 cm (3-4 ft) tall. For the front of the border, 'Fairy' can be very colourful in late summer and early autumn. It is a dwarf pompon chrysanthemum with numer ous round rosy-pink flowers. It grows to only 30 cm (1 ft).

To avoid winter losses of chrysanthemums, it is advisable to lift the stools (roots) in the autumn and house them in an airy cold frame. In spring take cuttings for rooting in the greenhouse. You will find new plants tend to flower more profusely than those grown from old roots.

Chrysanthemum maximum, (Shasta daisy), although quite a different flower, makes a good border plant. One of the best varieties is 'Esther Read' which grows 75 cm (2½ft) tall. Its large golden-eyed white flowers appear on long stems from June until August and are good for cutting. Propagate by root division in spring.

COREOPSIS*
Appreciated for their long flowering season (July-September) as long as they are given a position in full sun, these plants, commonly known as tickweed, are not fussy about soil type, although it must be well drained. *Coreopsis grandiflora* is a robust species from the U.S.A. that grows 45 cm (18 inches) high. Its leaves are narrow and deeply toothed and its bright yellow flowers measuring up to 7 cm (2½ inches) across, carried on good stems are first class for flower arrangements. *C. grandiflora verticillata* produces smaller flowers but more of them. Other named varieties include 'Badengold' which grows to 90 cm (3 ft) high and has pale yellow flowers, 'Perry's Variety' which grows to 75 cm (2½ft) high and has

semi-double yellow flowers; 'Sunray' which grows 45 cm (18 inches) high and is very free flowering with double golden yellow flowers; 'Mayfield Giant' which grows 60 cm (2 ft) high and is a golden yellow and 'Sunburst' also (2 ft) high and a bright yellow, semi-double variety.

Flowers can be grown from seed sown in May/July outdoors for flowering the follow-

The lovely blue flower spikes of delphinium

ing season, but propagation is best by division in the spring.

DELPHINIUM**
These are the aristrocrats of the herbaceous border and they are not difficult to grow if you start them off well. The first requirement is a deeply dug, well prepared soil. I en-

plant with a hard heel of the root. Put this in a jam jar containing 5 cm (2 inches) of sand and add water to come about 2.5 cm (1 inch) above the sand. Keep in a shaded, frost-free place. In four to five weeks, roots will have developed and the cuttings can be potted into 7.5–10 cm (3-4 inch) pots for planting out into their flowering positions in April/May.

DIANTHUS*
Pinks, Border Carnations

Whilst pinks and border carnations are listed here as perennials, after two or three years they do become untidy, producing weaker growth and poorer quality flowers, so it is best to replace them every second or third year with fresh plants. This is not difficult since they are easy to root either from cuttings taken between June and early August or by layering them in July and August. Whichever way you choose, propagating from young plants will give the best results. From pegging a layer down to rooting takes roughly six weeks. It is then time to sever the link with the mother plant and wait a further four weeks before lifting the new plant for its final planting out. Pinks and border carnation seed is readily available and should be sown thinly in a pan or box. Put in an unheated greenhouse or cold frame to germinate.

The growing plants need a sunny position in soil that is well drained. They favour a chalky soil, but failing this give a light application of garden lime prior to planting.

My first garden pinks were 'White Ladies', which have

---

sure this by digging the area in the winter, leaving the rough clods exposed to the elements. If the soil is inclined to be acid I apply a light dressing of garden lime before breaking down the clods in the spring. This winter exposure of the soil helps reduce the risk of subsequent slug damage to the dormant buds below ground. April/May is a good time to plant out but if the weather turns dry it will be necessary to water the plants until they are well established. Few garden plants grow faster than delphiniums and in consequence to get the finest blooms on healthy plants they need feeding and watering. I start by giving established plants an application of fertiliser towards the end of February – just about the time the new growth emerges. When the first flush of blooms has been cut down in July, I give a repeat application of fertiliser.

There are many named varieties of delphiniums and

The attractive flowers of bleeding heart, Dicentra spectabilis

in making your choice, it is important to take note of the heights they will reach. Staking and tying the taller ones will generally be necessary, especially if the garden is exposed. The tallest variety we have grown is 'Royal Marines' which reaches 2.4 metres (8 ft) and is dark purply blue. Our favourite, however, grows to only half this height. Called 'Clack's Choice' it has flowers that are a real delphinium blue colour, and as its stems are strong, it needs no staking.

Raising delphiniums from fresh seed is easy but as the seed ages germination results deteriorate. Storing seed in the refrigerator helps to slow down the deterioration. Sow the fresh seed in a seed bed in spring. Propagation from new cuttings taken early in the season is simple and successful. Using a very sharp knife cut a 10 cm (4 inch) shoot from the double white flower, and 'Mrs. Sinkins Pink'. Both of these have a glorious perfume. Of all the border carnations I have grown, 'Robin Thain' with its white striped rosy-crimson, clove-scented flowers is outstanding. Another old favourite is 'Zebra' which has maize-yellow flowers that are striped crimson. Also worth mentioning is 'Salmon Clove' which has soft salmon pink flowers that are delightfully perfumed. Pinks grow to about 30 cm (1 ft) high and generally do not need support to keep their blooms off the ground, but the border carnations, at twice or more this height, certainly will.

In between the border pinks and carnations there are the perpetual flowering hybrids, *Dianthus × allwoodii* which make truly wonderful garden plants. A particular favourite is 'Doris', which is a salmon pink colour with red eyes.

DICENTRA* Bleeding Heart
Growing some 75 cm (2½ ft) high, *D. spectabilis* is a tall, graceful plant. The rows of rose-pink and white heart-shaped flowers dangle from arching stems and are at their best in May and June. They are equally attractive in the flower bed or in a flower arrangement, and they are plants for that shady sheltered corner, away from the wind and the spring frosts. They can be grown from seed sown in May/June in pans protected from the weather in a frame. Seedlings should be potted singly in pots and planted out in spring in a planting site that has good drainage and some well-rotted compost incorporated. They can be propagated also by dividing lifted roots in March.

ECHINOPS* Globe Thistle
The globe thistles, with their round, prickly, ball-shaped flowerheads and dramatic grey and green foliage are always majestic plants during July and August. This is the time to cut and dry the flowers for winter use in flower arrangements. All varieties need plenty of space in a sunny well drained position. They can be grown from seed sown in April/July in open ground, or propagated by dividing the roots in October for overwintering in a cold frame. Plant out in March.

'Veitch's Blue' is a good dwarf variety, growing 75 cm (2½ ft) tall, and it has large deep blue flowerheads. 'Taplow Blue' produces steel-blue flowerheads which turn silvery with age. It grows 1.2 metres (4 ft) tall. *E. ritro*, growing to 1.35 metres (4½ ft) is appreciated for its soft blue flowerheads.

ERIGERON* Fleabane
A wide range of garden hybrids is now available, all of which succeed well in sunny borders and are not greatly perturbed if the soil is poor. The mauve and violet

Brightly coloured fleabane, Erigeron

flowered varieties are hardy, but the pink ones may die out during cold winters especially if the soil is poorly drained. All have a long flowering season, starting in June and going on until the autumn. The daisy like flowers last well when cut for indoor decoration.

The hardiest varieties include 'Darkest of All', which grows 45 cm (18 inches) high and has deep violet flowers with golden eyes; 'Dignity' which grows 60 cm (2 ft) tall and has flowers that are deep blue turning mauve and 'Sincerity' which grows 75 cm (2½ ft) tall and has flowers that are lilac mauve with a clear yellow centre. Those in the pink-rosy-carmine colour range include 'Foersters Liebling', growing to 60 cm (2 ft) tall with semi-double, rosy-carmine flowers and 'Gaiety' which grows 75 cm (2½ ft) tall and has large pink flowers.

Plants can be grown from seed sown in April/May in a cold frame for planting out in October or March, or by dividing the roots in March.

EUPHORBIA* Spurge
This genus of about 2000 species is widely distributed throughout the world. For the flower garden however, we are only concerned with the hardy herbaceous or sub-shrubby members of the family. The flowers of euphorbia are small and insignificant; it is the surrounding petal-like bracts that create the beauty. At Clack's Farm we get the best results for these plants when grown in our poorest and driest soil areas and it doesn't matter whether they are in sun or partial shade.

The popular and colourful fuchsia

E. *Polychroma* is outstanding; growing to 45 cm (18 inches), it produces brilliant yellow bracts in early spring akin to a touch of sunlight. E. *Wulfenii* grows to 75 cm (2½ ft) and has glaucous foliage and yellowish-green spikes appearing in May. E. *Griffithii* 'Fireglow' grows to 45 cm (1½ ft) and has orange-red bracts and pinky foliage. It remains splendid from May/July. Euphorbia can be grown from seed sown in April/June in a cold frame or outdoors, for

planting out in the following autumn. Alternatively, propagate by dividing the roots in March/April or by taking soft wood cuttings in April/June.

FUCHSIA**
This is probably among the most popular of all plants. Although it is seldom used as a hardy perennial, with some extra care several varieties can be left in the flower bed during the winter.

When starting to grow fuchsias obtain advice and plants from a good fuchsia nursery. Taking cuttings is easy and best done during May/June. These should be overwintered in a frost-free greenhouse so that they grow into healthy young plants. Plant these out at the end of May, putting them as deep as is practicable in the ground. This is the best protection you can give the plant against winter frost damage. Cut them back in November and put a layer of compost, and if need be, bracken or straw, on top to protect the plants further. With nearly all varieties, new growth will come from the roots in April/May and plants will start flowering from July/August. Regular feeding and watering during dry spells is essential for maintaining healthy and vigorous plants. They tolerate any soil as long as it is moisture retentive.

'Mrs. Popple' is one of the hardiest varieties together with 'Riccartonii' but many others such as 'Celia Smedley', 'Madame Cornelissen' and 'Tom Thumb' do well.

GAILLARDIA*
Blanket Flower
The garden hybrids are plants for hot sunny borders, but they do not have a long life, particularly when a cold wet winter intervenes. A well drained soil is essential and if it is light so much the better. Spring is the time to plant these flowers, certainly no later than early May. Propagation is by division of roots in March/April or by root cuttings taken in January and kept in a cold greenhouse or frame. Plants can also be grown from seed sown outdoors in May/June. The seedlings should be thinned and

left to grow into healthy plants ready for planting out the following March/April.

The following are a few of the colourful varieties that will flower from July till September: 'Burgundy' which grows 60 cm (2 ft) high and has red flowers; 'Mandarin' which grows 90 cm (3 ft) high and has bright rusty orange flowers that have no yellow eye and 'Wirral Flame' which grows 90 cm (3 ft) high and has flowers that are a deep rusty red with a yellow edge. It is advisable to provide twiggy supports around the plants early in the season otherwise the flower stems tend to flop over in the slightest wind.

Gentiana sino-ornata

GENTIANA**
This family of plants come from high altitude alpine regions where the winter snows cover and protect them from frost, where the peaty soils are moist during the growing season and where the air is always clean and the summer sunshine intensely bright. It is these factors that have to be considered if gentians are to be introduced successfully into our gardens, for failure to give them something akin to their natural environment is sure to produce poor and disappointing results. Having said that, it is possible to achieve success by preparing pockets of moist peaty or leaf mould soils amongst the stones in a sunny rock garden. As a substitute

for winter snow, a raised sheet of glass over each plant will prevent them suffering from root damage caused by winter water-logging.

My favourites are G. *acaulis*, the blue trumpet gentian which flowers in May/June, G. *sino-ornata* with its brilliant blue flowers in September/October, and the autumn-flowering G. × *macaulayi*.

Plants can be propagated either from root cuttings taken in April/May or by division of plants in March, G. *acaulis* should be divided in June).

Fresh seed sown in late summer and subjected to winter freezing in a cold frame generally germinates well.

GERANIUM* Cranesbill

This is a large family of hardy summer-flowering perennial plants which are very different from bedding geraniums. So varied are they in size and growth habits that some of the tall ones can be planted in herbaceous borders to advantage whilst other low growing varieties are more suitable for rock gardens. The whole family is happiest when the soil is well drained and not too rich. In such conditions the plants should be liberally smothered with blooms.

G. *psilostemon*, growing to 75 cm (2½ ft) high has numerous magenta red flowers with black centres and veins. In addition it has beautifully coloured leaves in autumn. It likes a position in full sun. G. *pratense*, (the meadow geranium) grows 60 cm (2 ft) high and is available in several colours from white to violet blue; the one I particularly like is 'Flore Peano' with its double

blue flowers. G. *macrorrhizum* 'Ingwersen's' variety is shade tolerant and often used as ground cover as it only grows to 30 cm (1 ft) high. It has soft pink flowers and masses of aromatic leaves which colour beautifully in autumn. For the rock garden try the low-growing G. *cinereum* 'Ballerina' which reaches only 7.5–15 cm (3-6 inches) high and has pale rosy purple flowers deeply veined with crimson.

Propagation is by division of plants in March.

GEUM*

Given the right conditions – that is a fairly rich soil in full sun – geums make a colourful contribution to the flower garden for most of the summer. To keep them in good flowering health, it is advisable to lift and divide the roots every second or third year. Early spring is the best time either for planting or re-planting, and the plants like a little really well-rotted compost underneath them.

The varieties I have been pleased to grow are: 'Mrs. Bradshaw' which grows to 60 cm (2 ft) high, and with its double flaming brick red flowers, is an old favourite of mine; 'Lady Stratheden' which grows 60 cm (2 ft) high and has semi-double, warm yellow flowers and 'Fire Opal' which grows 75 cm (2 ft) high and also has semi-double flowers, that are orange-scarlet with purple stems.

Plants can be raised from seed sown in a cold frame from April to July for planting out the following spring or by division of the roots in March/April.

GYPSOPHILA*
Chalk Plant

This is planted in small numbers to supply material for cut flower arrangements, particularly to go with sweet peas and carnations in July/August. It is at this time that the delicate sprays of tiny flowers are quite beautiful and make every vase or bowl look a professional arrangement. The plants grow best in full sun on chalky soils; on other soil types an application of garden lime before planting is advisable. To get the best effect allow the plants adequate space to spread out their flowering branches without crowding. A free-standing plant in full bloom becomes a glorious hazy cloud of colour. Once planted they should not be disturbed.

'Bristol Fairy' which grows 1.2 metres (4 ft) high is my favourite and is probably the best double white for cutting; it is also a good strong grower. The pale pink-flowered 'Rosy Veil' is a different type; growing only 45 cm (1½ ft) high, it has a low spreading habit.

Propagation can be achieved by root cuttings taken in May/June and rooted in sand or a rooting bag. G. *paniculata* which grows 75 cm (2½ ft) tall, can be grown from seed sown in the greenhouse in February/April. It should be kept at a temperature between 10°-15°C (50°-60°F).

HELENIUM* Sneezeweed

This could be described as one of our best herbaceous plants. It thrives in a poor soil and simply loves a hot summer. Under these conditions, the 90 cm (3 ft) stems are hard and strong and stand well without

support. By planting several varieties, the flowering season can cover the four months from July to October. In common with many other perennials, the flowering quality is maintained by lifting, dividing and replanting every other year.

To start the season we grow 'Moerheim Beauty' which flowers in July/August and reaches a height of 90 cm (3 ft). There is considerable warmth in its large crimson-red, daisy like flowers, which have a dark centre. Another for July/August flowering is 'Coppelia', which grows 90 cm (3 ft) high and has coppery-orange flowers. For flowering in August/September, 'Bruno' has really deep crimson-red flowers with a dark centre. It grows to 90 cm (3 ft). After that try 'Butterpat' which also grows 90 cm (3 ft) tall and has

bright yellow flowers that remain into October. The earlier flowering varieties, such as 'Moerheim Beauty' will sometimes produce a second flush of flowers in October if cut down immediately after the first crop is finished.

As always I prefer early spring planting. Propagation is by division of roots in early spring.

HELIANTHEMUM*
Rock Rose

For a display of colour in June and July plant these rock roses. They never fail to brighten up a flower garden, particularly if given the benefit of full sunshine and good drainage. They are most at home in a sunny rock garden, where they will quickly demand more and more space. After flowering therefore, it is wise to trim the plants back

Rosy clouds of pale pink-flowered Gypsophila 'Rosy Veil'

drastically. This annual pruning gives rise to the production of new vigorous growth for flowering again later in the season.

Some of the best named varieties are 'Ben Afflick', which has orange and buff flowers; 'Beech Park Scarlet' which, true to its name, is a crimson scarlet; 'Wisley Pink' – a delightful pink, and 'Wisley Primrose' – a soft yellow. Planting out time is September to March when the soil is not frosted.

Propagation is done by taking 7.5 cm (3 inch) cuttings of non-flowering growth with a heel from June to August. Overwinter newly rooted plants in a cold frame and plant out in March when it is getting warmer.

HELLEBORUS*
Christmas and Lenten Rose

It is surprising how few hellebores are needed to bring considerable life and joy to a flower garden in winter and early spring. It is such a thrill to have two or three Christmas Roses (*Helleborus niger*) as a centre piece on the dinner table at Christmas time, that it is worth all the trouble of using cloches and dealing with the slugs to get them in bloom for that special occasion. All our hellebores do fine in shade or semi-shade where the soil is moist. We leave them alone as much as possible so as to avoid the slightest disturbance of their roots, but give them a little fertiliser feed after flowering. By hand-weeding around the plants we get quite a few self-sown seedlings.

There are several forms of the Christmas Rose – some with very much larger flowers than others. We favour Potter's Wheel, which has pure white, broad petals with no pink flush on the back of them. If protected with a cloche against the weather and slugs, this variety will give perfect blooms for Christmas, but be prepared to wait a couple of years or so for the plant to settle down before it decides to produce flowers. *Helleborus orientalis*, the Lenten Rose, produces several large nodding flowers on each stem from February to April. It gives us so much pleasure, particularly as we now have numbers of seedlings, each with a different arrangement of colours, from deep purple to creamy white petals with or without spots inside. If, after cutting, you dip the flower

stalk ends in boiling water for a second or two and then stand the flowers up to their necks in water overnight, you will find that they keep so much longer in an arrangement. *Helleborus corsicus* grows to 60 cm (2 ft) and makes quite a large plant. Its strong stems carry creamy-green flower trusses from early February until May. Not only are the flower heads sought after by flower arrangers but the seed heads that follow are just as interesting for the same purpose. *Helleborus foetidus*, Stinking Hellebore, grows to 45 cm (18 inches). A native of this country, it produces its flower heads from February to April, followed again by attractive seed heads.

All hellebores are beloved by whitefly and greenfly so preventive spraying is essential. Best planting time is March. Propagation is by division of roots in March or seedlings planted out at that time.

HEMEROCALLIS*
Day Lily

These easily grown plants have a unique flower production system; during the flowering season a single flower on each stem opens in the morning and dies at night to be followed by a new fresh bloom on the same stem the next day. This flowering routine goes on without a break for six to eight weeks and by growing several varieties of the best garden hybrids it is possible to have these beautiful lily flowers from May until August. The plants do well in most soils, either in partial shade or sun.

To start the flowering season in May/June, plant 'Gold

Dust' which grows to 45 cm (18 inches) tall and has yellow flowers with a dark reverse. Follow with 'Tejas' which grows to 75 cm (2½ft). Its bright coppery-crimson flowers appear in June/July. If you prefer a clear yellow flower plant 'Hyperion' instead; it grows to 90 cm (3 ft). For July/August, you could choose from 'Bonanza' which grows to 45 cm (18 inches) high and has flowers that are buff yellow with a dark brown throat or 'Mrs John Tigert', which grows 75 cm (2½ft) tall and has coppery-red flowers with a dark centre. At the end of the flowering season cut the stems down to ground level.

Propagation is by division of roots between October and March. Once planted take care not to disturb the roots.

HOSTA* Plantain Lily

The bold, spade-shaped leaves in many shades of grey, green and sometimes almost blue or golden yellow, with or without contrasting margins, make hostas great plants not only for the flower gardener but also for those interested in flower arranging. These plants thrive particularly well in partial shade provided by close shrubs or trees, and where the soil is cool and moist; nearby the edge of a pool or pond is a good spot. In such conditions they will go on producing leaf upon leaf to make ever-enlarging plants from the time they wake up in the spring until late autumn. In addition to their magnificent foliage, they do grace the garden with upright spikes of delicate lilac, lily-like flowers. In shady conditions the foliage generally grows better, whereas if the plants are in full sun, there tends to be a better crop of flowers.

There are certainly too many varieties of hosta to list here, but two outstanding ones are: *Hosta fortunei* 'Albopicta' which has yellow leaves edged with pale green (in fact there are several *fortunei* varieties in different combinations of green and yellow) and *Hosta sieboldiana* with lovely blue-grey crinkled, and deeply veined leaves.

Propagation is by division of the clumps in spring; the divided plants must be replanted at once. When the weather is dry, water the newly planted plants regularly. Hosta can also be grown from

The Christmas rose, Helleborus niger

seed sown in April/May, but remember that each plant will be an individual and will probably not be the same as the parent plant.

IBERIS* Candytuft

These small, evergreen, 'no-trouble' plants are so easy to grow; they ask simply for ordinary soil and a dry sunny position. *Iberis saxalitis* reaches some 10-15 cm (4-6 inches) in height and is a spreading plant, well suited for a rock garden. The white flat flower heads make a good show in May/June. *Iberis sempervirens*, growing 15-23 cm (6-9 inches) is taller and makes a larger spreading plant, reaching anything up to 60 cm (2 ft) across. It is more suitable for planting on top of a dry wall or for general open situations. Two other good varieties are

'Little Gem' and 'Snow Flake' growing 15 cm (6 inches) and 23 cm (9 inches) tall respectively. Both have white flowers.

Propagation of named varieties is by heel cuttings taken after flowering.

IRIS* Bearded Iris

This is the June-flowering iris, commonly known as Flag Iris. For the best results, give them a position in full sunshine with good drainage. Any waterlogging will be fatal. They are at their happiest on chalky soils; on other soil types additional garden lime is necessary. It is advisable to apply a general garden fertiliser at the beginning of the growing season. On all soils deficiencies of calcium and phosphates in the soil results in poor plant health and in extreme cases, death of the plants.

Although the flowering season of iris is short, whilst it lasts the display of colour and beauty will always be spectacular, especially if you select the varieties you grow carefully. There are so many varieties to choose from, that rather than name a few I suggest you consult a specialist's catalogue, or better still make a visit to a nearby nursery in June to see those that they have in flower. In addition to the taller varieties and hybrids there are many dwarf ones, some of which only grow to 10 cm (4 inches) high.

For all varieties the best planting time is October. Set the solid rhizome, (bought initially from a nursery) into the planting hole so that the upper side is exposed to the sun; deeper planting can result in the rhizome rotting. To propagate irises, divide established healthy rhizomes soon after flowering; select outer pieces which each have a good strong leaf fan and then clip the fan to half its size before planting, discarding the old centre. To maintain plant health and free-flowering, replant in this way every third year.

KNIPHOFIA*
Torch Lily, Red Hot Poker
These are plants that do best in full sunshine on well-drained soils. Shade reduces flowering and winter water-logging causes plant losses. To keep the plants in good flowering condition, apply an organic fertiliser around them in April. Continuity of flowering can be achieved by cutting the stems down close to the base when they have finished flowering. On heavy soils or in cold, wet

areas, it is advisable to provide some protection against possible frost damage, such as covering the roots with straw or bracken. To reduce possible winter damage, I would always recommend planting in the spring rather than the autumn. When planting, do make sure that the planting hole is large enough for the roots to be well spread out.

Of the many varieties, 'Samuel's Sensation', which grows 1.5 metres (5 ft) high, is outstanding with its bright red-scarlet blooms. 'Bressingham Torch' growing to 90 cm (3 ft) is also spectacular and has orange-yellow spikes. Propagation is by division of established plants in April.

LAVANDULA* Lavender
It is difficult to imagine any flower garden without at least one or two well cared for lavender plants. On a summer day, their masses of perfumed flower spikes are glorious. To grow lavender well, an adequately drained soil is needed. If it is slightly chalky so much the better; for success, just plant in a full sunshine position. If the soil is light and inclined to be acid an annual application of garden lime is beneficial. Lavender is generally short lived, but trimming back and tidying up the plants, cutting away all the dead flower spikes each year in March or April, does tend to keep them in good health for longer.

The Old English Lavender (*Lavandula spica*), renowned for its fragrant essential oil, is still popular in spite of the fact that its height – it grows to 90 cm (3 ft) – means it needs

plenty of space. Its blue-purple flower spikes bloom from July to September. The dwarf variety, 'Munstead', growing to 45 cm (18 inches) is my favourite with its deep mauve spikes of flowers, and it is undoubtedly good for an average-sized garden. 'Hidcote' is another compact variety and has dark violet flowers. If you want to dry stems of flowers, cut these when the flowers are just showing colour but not fully open. The fragrance is then retained at its best.

Propagation is easy; take 7.5 cm (3 inch) cuttings of ripe non-flowering shoots, and when rooted overwinter them in a cold frame. Plant out in March or April.

LUPINUS* Lupin
Apart from the tree lupin *Lupinus arboreus* – which incidentally is a plant well worth growing from seed – today's hybrid garden lupins are the result of dedicated breeding work. The world famous Russell strain are lupins with strong stems, plenty of vigour and clear colours in every flower, usually with two distinct colours in each one. One of the first lupins I grew was 'Elsie Waters', bright pink and cream with white edges, a sensation at that time. There are still many named varieties available.

Lupins are at their best in a light, lime-free soil with no manure added. All Russell lupins grow to about 105 cm (3½ ft) and flower in June/early July. If the dead flower spikes are removed before seed formation, flowering will resume in a limited way. Propagation of named varieties is done by cuttings taken with a heel in April. Alternatively sow mixed seeds in May/June in a frame for planting out in October. These plants will then flower the following summer.

MECONOPSIS**
Himalayan Poppy, Welsh Poppy

There are many species of these hardy perennials, all of which have poppy-like flowers. For me, the exciting ones are those with blue flowers that give us so much pleasure in June and July. To grow them successfully, provide them with the right conditions – a light rich, moist soil that is always moist but nevertheless well-drained in a spot that is sheltered and semi-shaded. In addition, they need plenty of water during the summer and – ideally – as little winter rain as possible. In wet districts it would be advisable to cover the roots with cloches immediately after cutting down the dead flower stems. Throughout late autumn and winter, the roots are completely dormant with no sign of life above ground.

Meconopsis betonicifolia (syn *M. Baileyi*), the Himalayan blue poppy, is the one with those delightful sky blue flowers and bright yellow anthers, and it is well worth that extra bit of tender loving care demanded to grow it successfully. It reaches a height of 90 cm (3 ft). *M. grandis* produces its dark blue, almost purple with a tinge of red, flowers slightly earlier in May/June. The yel-

Russell lupins in full flower

61

low varieties, *M. cambrica* (Welsh poppy) and *M. integrifolia*, are attractive but can become a nuisance as they seed very freely. The seeds are easy to harvest but should then be sown immediately as they quickly lose their germination qualities. With fresh seed germination takes two to three weeks. When the seedlings can be handled, prick them out into trays and overwinter in a cold frame. The seedlings also go completely dormant; do not despair, they are not dead but just resting. In the spring, growth will recommence, at which time they can be planted outside. The plants can also be propagated by division in March/April.

NEPETA* Catmint
This attractive aromatic plant, with its blue-grey foliage and misty mauve flower spikes, is often used as an edging plant. It does well on light soils in full

The pretty, papery yellow flowers of the Welsh poppy, Meconopsis cambrica

sun but on heavy, cold, poorly drained soils, it tends to die out fairly quickly.

Nepeta mussinii, which grows to 45 cm (18 inches) high, is the species commonly grown, but the variety 'Six Hills Giant', which grows to 60 cm (2 ft) and has violet-blue flowers, makes a better and more positive display. However, it is sterile and therefore cannot be grown from seed.

Propagation is by division of roots in spring or by soft cuttings taken after flowering. *N. mussinii* can be grown from seed sown outside in May/June.

PAEONIA* Paeony
There are several different types of paeonies including the old-fashioned, cottage gar-

den types with their green foliage and scented double flowers. The double Chinese paeonies are now very popular; they have a greater range of delightful colours and the added virtue of being scented. There are also the single Japanese and Imperial paeonies, which have cupped blooms of five to ten petals, each with a cluster of yellow stamens. Unfortunately, however, all of these are somewhat weaker growers.

Paeonies need plenty of sunshine and well-prepared ground with some well-rotted compost or manure incorporated. Some of the better perfumed varieties are subject to spring frost damage which can spoil the opening flower buds, so if possible, plant them in such a position that they escape early morning spring sunshine. After planting paeonies in the spring considerable patience is needed as they may take several years before showing any sign of flowering. Established plants benefit considerably from an annual springtime mulch, again with the well-rotted compost or with manure.

Amongst the old cottage paeonies, (*P. officinalis*), which grow to 45 cm (18 inches) tall, there are 'Alba-plena' – a double white; 'Rosea-plena' – a double pink and 'Rubra-plena' – a double crimson. All flower in May/June. Among the many excellent double Chinese paeonies, all of which flower in June, are: 'Adolph Rousseau' – a crimson; 'Alex Fleming' – bright rose-pink; 'Kelway's Glorious' – pure white and 'President Wilson' – pale cream pink. Single bloom varieties include 'Globe of Light' – a pink with a large cream-yellow centre; 'Jan van Leeuwen' – pure white with a golden centre and 'Soshi' – rose with a yellow centre.

Propagation is done by division of roots in September or early October. Once planted, on no account disturb the roots. With no disturbance paeonies will live thirty years or more, progressively making larger roots and flowering more prolific.

PENSTEMON*

These graceful plants, with their 60-90 cm (2-3 ft) tall spikes of open-mouthed flowers appearing from July to September, are well worth a place in any garden. They are short lived, however, so frequent replacement is necessary, but being easy to grow this does not present any real problems. Plant in the spring, giving them a place in the sun where the soil is well-drained. 'Garnet' is just about the hardiest of the large-flowered penstemons. It makes a neat bushy plant and produces spikes of super crimson flowers. 'Firebird' has the same growth habit but its flowers are bright scarlet. Various seed mixtures are available such as 'Grandiflorum Excelsior' which grows to 75 cm (2½ ft), or 'Skyline' which has a more bushy growth habit. Both have a lovely mixture of colours.

Sow seed outside in a seed bed from June to August and transplant to flowering positions in October. The plants will flower the following season. Propagation can also be done by division in the spring.

PHLOX*

These are undoubtedly the plants to grow for a late summer colour display, although they need looking after. They need a rich, well-cultivated soil and one that is capable of holding its moisture during the growing season. Failing this, some artificial watering during dry periods is necessary. Eelworm in phlox can become a problem, especially

if they have grown on the same ground for many years. Because of this, it is always wise to plant fresh healthy stock on ground where phlox have not been grown in recent years. If possible select a sunny or slightly shaded position, prepare the ground thoroughly with either well-rotted com-

A magnificent double white paeony

post or manure and then plant out in the spring. Replace with young healthy plants every three or four years. All phlox are prone to suffer from mildew but early spraying will control this.

My own choice of varieties include 'Cinderella' which has lilac-pink flowers with rose eyes and grows to 90 cm (3 ft) tall; 'Firefly' which grows to 75 cm (2½ ft) tall and has pink flowers with crimson eyes; 'Rembrandt' which is pure white and grows 90 cm (3 ft) tall and 'San Antonio' which is claret red and grows 75 cm (2½ ft) tall. The only variegated type, with pale mauve flowers, is 'Norah Leigh' and it grows 60 cm (2 ft) tall. It is a really bright choice for the border, although it is a slow grower.

Root cuttings taken in March and grown on will be ready for planting out the following spring, but only propagate from healthy plants.

PHYSALIS*
Chinese Lantern
These plants are usually grown for the ornamental calix which looks like an inflated orange balloon. If cut whilst the colour is still good, the stems of lanterns can be dried for winter indoor decoration, but remove the foliage first. Before the puffy green balloons change colour in late autumn, they can be used to advantage in flower arrangements.

Spring is the best time to plant these flowers; do so in a sunny or partially shady situation where the soil is well drained. Keep a careful eye on the plant as it grows; it is not

only invasive with its roots, but it also self-seeds freely.

Propagation is by division of the long fleshy roots or by seed sown from May to July in a cold frame. The resulting plants can be planted out in spring the following season.

POLYGONATUM*
Solomon's Seal
Solomon's Seal, *P. multiflorum*, is one of the easiest plants to grow in a border. Although it is not at all particular about the type of soil in which it grows, we have found that ours do well with their roots in the shade and their arching stems in semi-shade. In May and June, the white-waisted flowers in clusters of two or three, hang gracefully down almost along the full length of each stem. They are set off by a background of equi-spaced oblong mid-green leaves, which turn a lovely shade of yellow in the autumn.

Propagation is by division of rhizomes in March/April or from small rhizome eyes potted on and kept in a cold frame or greenhouse until large enough to be planted out.

PRIMULA*
From a vast number of species collected in the Southern hemisphere, there are fortunately some that have proved to be hardy enough to tolerate the varying conditions in our flower gardens. Generally speaking, they behave best when the soil is cool and moist throughout the whole year, which is why most of them are happier in the northern half of the country. Our native primrose (*P. vulgaris*) is still one of the finest garden plants; if you

can, give it a place on a heavy loam grassy bank in semi-shade and then leave it undisturbed to establish itself. The ever popular purple-red version, *P. vulgaris* 'Wanda' is far less fussy in its growing requirements. A recent introduction, *P. vulgaris* 'Sue Jervis', with shell-pink flowers, is also worth trying. All these flower in March/April.

Polyanthus, with their trusses of primrose-like flowers produced on stout stems, are all garden hybrids, well known and appreciated for their colourful displays in the spring. We have found 'Pacific Strain' particularly successful. For borders, members of the 'candelabra' group can be recommended. Most of these have whorls of flowers arranged on their elongated stems. Our choice includes 'Bullyana' – shades of orange; 'Japonica' hybrids – a mixture of crimson, rose and white, 'Pulverulenta' – rosy-purple – and one we particularly would not be without, 'Florindae', which was jokingly called by a visitor 'a cowslip on a stick'. All flower between May and July. *Primula denticulata* (drumstick primrose) is now available in several colours – varying from pale lilac to deep purple and rose pink to crimson, as well as pure white.

All primulas can be grown from seed, but this should be as fresh as possible. Sow from May to August in trays and cover with glass or plastic sheeting to prevent drying out. Keep in a fairly cool place; high temperatures impair germination. The plants can also be propagated by division of roots after flowering.

PULSATILLA*
Pasque Flower
Sometimes known as *Anemone pulsatilla*, it is difficult to believe that this exquisitely beautiful plant, *P. vulgaris*, was once a weed of our West Country pastures. Now it is regarded as one of the garden treasures. It has mid-green flower buds, which open to cup-shaped, pale lilac flowers. These are followed by glorious seed heads. We grow it in a

Physalis, the Chinese lantern

sunny position, where, during the autumn it dies down completely to come back to life in March. It does best on well-drained soils, especially if given a little garden lime.

As the plants are difficult to grow from division, it is best to start with seed which should be as fresh as possible. Sow this outdoors in August. Seed of hybrids in mixed colours is available, but bear in mind that some of the red hybrids are rather less vigorous than the original plant.

PYRETHRUM*
Excellent plants for a sunny border, these do best on light, well-drained soils where slugs are not a problem. Their large daisy-like flowers with golden 'button' centres, brighten up the garden continually from May until August. It is advisable to provide some support to prevent the slender flower stems being blown over; a few twigs pushed into the ground around each plant early in the spring will suffice. During drought periods watering will be necessary to maintain growth of foliage and flowers, but do start well before the plants show any signs of wilting.

There are numerous good varieties to choose from. I can recommend 'E.M. Robinson' – a pale pink, 'James Kelway' – a crimson red, and 'Marjorie Robinson' – a deep pink.

Propagation is by division of the roots in the spring and that is also the time for planting bought-in stock. Autumn planting can result in considerable losses. Large-flowered hybrids may be raised from seed sown in June/July outside or in a cold frame.

RUDBECKIA* Cone Flower
These are invaluable plants for a late summer show of colour. They like a well-drained prepared soil with adequate drainage in an open sunny position. In exposed situations some form of support is advisable, or else the flower stems are inclined to get spread-eagled in high winds. Of the many available varieties, I would suggest 'Goldquelle', which, with its bushy habit, grows to 75 cm

(2½ft) high and has large double yellow flowers that bloom from July to October; 'Goldsturm', which grows to 60cm (2ft) and has flowers with long deep golden yellow petals surrounding a black centre, appearing from July until September, and R. newmanii 'Speciosa' which is the original 'Black-Eyed Susan' having yellow flowers with black centres, appearing on branching stems from July until September.

Propagation is by division of the roots in spring and excellent plants can be raised from seed sown outside from March to May.

SALVIA* Sage

The hardy perennial sages are not what I would call exciting plants, but, nevertheless, some varieties are undoubtedly worthy of a place in a large border. Being relatively short-lived plants and untidy in old age, replacement is advisable every few years and they should also be trimmed back each autumn. All varieties do best when planted in an open sunny position.

Salvia haematodes grows to a height of 90cm (3ft) and has graceful branching spikes of lavender blue flowers. It is one of the most popular varieties for June/July flowering. Salvia superba grows to a height of 75cm (2½ft) and makes a bushy plant with violet-purple flowers that appear in July/August. Salvia superba 'Lubeco' at 45cm (18 inches) tall is a shorter more compact plant. The foliage of all has an aromatic scent.

Propagation is by cuttings with a heel taken during the late summer and overwintered in a cold frame for planting out the following spring. Alternatively you can sow seed in August/September in the greenhouse.

SCABIOSA*

Scabious, Pincushion Flower

These really splendid plants for cut flowers all have a long flowering season – from June to September – if the dead heads are removed regularly. To grow them successfully a thoroughly prepared soil which has had an application of garden lime is needed. They will not do so well on acid soils. The ever popular 'Clive Greaves', which grows 90cm (3ft) high, produces a constant supply of large lavender blue flowers on long stems which do not require staking. 'Miss Wilmott' with its white flowers has similar growth habit and the relatively new 'Lucida' has pink flowers above dark green foliage.

Propagation is by division of roots in the spring or by cuttings taken with a heel after flowering. Planting out should always be done in the spring.

SEDUM*

Stone Crop, Ice Plant

These late-flowering semi-succulents S. spectabile, with glaucous green foliage are beloved by the butterflies and bees in the autumn. For the sake of both plants and butterflies, it is best to plant them in full sunshine. Being fairly rapid growers they need space to spread out so they can display their rosy-purple large flat flowerheads to their best.

The variety, 'Autumn Joy', is well named; its flowers open to a salmon pink and go on changing colour until the end of the season. It grows to a height of 60cm (2ft). The dwarf variety, 'September Ruby', growing only to 30cm (1ft), has deep rose-pink flowerheads.

Propagation is easy; stem cuttings taken in June/July will seldom fail.

SOLIDAGO* Golden Rod

These are so easy to grow that they are often neglected and as a result become poor plants. Being gross feeders they do need a feed of general fertiliser each spring to keep them in good trim. They undoubtedly do best in full sun, but will tolerate partial shade. The taller varieties may need staking to prevent them flopping over when fully grown. As with most perennials the old flower stems should be cut down in October/November.

Some of the newer varieties I would recommend are: 'Cloth of Gold', which grows to 45cm (18 inches) and makes a robust plant with deep yellow flower heads; 'Crown of Rays', which grows to the same height and has attractive horizontal golden spikes; 'Golden Thumb', which grows to 30cm (1ft) and is a neat plant with yellow fluffy flowerheads, and the tall 'Mimosa', which grows 1.5 metres (5ft) high and is a trouble-free plant with yellow flowerheads.

Propagation is by division of roots which should be done in March/April. Plants can also be grown from seed which you should sow in a cold frame in March.

VERBASCUM* Mullein

These rather short-lived plants always capture attention especially when they flower majestically as individual plants in a garden. They are so stately looking, often towering above their surrounding neighbours to show off their long, thick and sometimes woolly spires of flowers which appear in July/August. They really are a must for any flower garden, even if you only grow a single plants. They love the sun and are not deterred by drought.

'Cotswold Queen' grows 1.3 metres (4½ ft) high and has branching stems and buff-orange flowers. 'Gainsborough' grows 1.2 metres (4 ft) high and is the most beautiful of them all with its graceful, spikes of clear yellow flowers. Unfortunately it is beautiful of them all with its graceful spikes of clear yellow high and has branching stems to carry its pure white flowers above the felty green leaves.

Propagation of named varieties is by taking 7.5 cm (3 inch) long cuttings in March for rooting in a cold frame, or from root cuttings taken in December/January. To grow from seed, sow 'Choice' mixed in April/June outside for flowering the following year.

VERONICA* Speedwell

This is a useful and attractive border plant, which given a well-drained soil enriched with some well-rotted compost and a place in full sun or partial shade will be very happy. *Veronica gentianoides* grows 60 cm (2 ft) high and is sometimes planted for ground cover. It produces slender

spikes of palest grey-blue flowers in April/May. *Veronica incana* 'Saraband' grows 45 cm (18 inches) high and has beautiful grey foliage followed by violet-blue flowers that appear from June to August. *Veronica spicata* 'Barcarolle', grows to 45 cm (18 inches) and makes a neat carpet of dark foliage punctuated with narrow spikes of deep rose-pink flowers in June/July. *V. spicata* 'Red Fox', grows to 37 cm (15 inches) and has red flowers

Veronica gentianoides, speedwell

from June to September.

All named varieties can be propagated from lateral cuttings taken in July/August. They should be rooted in a cold frame and potted on for planting out the following March.

Veronica teucrium 'Shirley Blue' can be grown from seed sown in May to July outside to flower the following season. It grows to 30 cm (1 ft).

ROSES

It is impossible for me to imagine a flower garden, however small or large without at least a few roses. Whatever variation the seasons may bring, roses never fail to greet the early summer days of June with the splendour of their glorious, colourful blooms. If a careful choice of varieties is made the delight of perfume will come as an extra bonus.

There are literally hundreds of varieties to choose from, but as their growth and flowering habits vary greatly the first thing to do is to decide on the type of rose plants you want to grow. Bush roses, for example are divided into two groups, Hybrid Teas (H.T.s) which produce large individual blooms on single stems, and Floribundas whose characteristic of many blooms produced in clusters or trusses has made them very popular for mass colour displays. Both Hybrid Teas and Floribundas can also be grown as standards; in this instance they flower on a 90 cm (3 ft) single stem which will need a strong stake for support.

For covering pergolas, walls or fences, roses with vigorous growth habits are needed. These are classified as climbing or rambling roses, of which the older varieties will flower only once during the summer. Some of the more recent additions, however, provide repeat displays of blooms throughout or later on in the season. Some of the modern shrub roses, too, have the same repeat-flowering qualities and merit consideration, not only as individual plants in a bed or border but also for planting as flowering hedges. Their useful deterrent of thorns against vandals – human or otherwise – make them particularly effective when grown as a hedge.

After several false starts, miniature roses which almost live up to their classification, have been produced. They can be expected to grow to about 45 cm (18 inches) high and produce miniature flowers in great quantity. Grown in small containers or pots, where their root growth is restricted, they can do extremely well. Provided they are watered and fed regularly, they prove good value for money. Amongst the miniatures, there are a few varieties with prostrate or semi-prostrate growth habits. These have been segregated and termed 'Ground Cover Roses'. Whilst we have been delighted to have them at Clack's Farm, the term ground cover can be somewhat misleading. We found the weeds loved the shelter provided and because of the thorns on the roses, weeding has become fairly painful.

The first golden rule for success with roses will always be the preparation of the soil before planting. A heavy clay soil, which is the best type for growing roses, often lacks good drainage; digging in of home-made, well-rotted compost or a mixture of peat and sand will improve it. With lighter soils it is advisable to step up the water-holding capacity by digging in well-rotted compost or farmyard manure. If neither of these is available, use peat on its own.

Another golden rule is to plant your roses in the sunniest position possible; they will repay you royally for giving them the best place in the garden. Feed them regularly with a rose fertiliser, first in March, followed by a repeat application in early June. If you can get some farmyard manure to use as a top dressing early in March, your roses will be more than grateful. It will certainly give a lift to the overall health of the plants, improving the foliage and the quality of the blooms.

PRUNING ROSES
The pruning of roses is a controversial subject. Whilst the third week in March is often suggested as the correct time, I have for years pruned our bush roses before Christmas and, by so doing, have been able to contain the black spot problem simply because all the old dead infected foliage is then out of the way. I prune them down to two or three buds above the ground in late autumn; it is important to make a clean cut on a slant so that water cannot collect on the top of the stem causing it to rot. Then in early spring, I remove any wood that has died back. Make sure that your secateurs are really sharp so that you achieve a clean cut without crushing the wood. Bush roses should also be pruned just after their first flowering to encourage a second flush of blooms.

Climbing, rambling and shrub roses should be pruned at the end of their flowering season as they all flower on old wood. Climbers and ramblers should be pruned back to a framework of healthy wood; with shrub roses, it is wise to cut out all the thin straggly growth and cut the strong wood back by one-third.

PROPAGATING ROSES

You can propagate favourite roses by taking cuttings of them in August. Select strong shoots of the current season's growth and cut a 18-20 cm (7-8 inch) length of stem cleanly below a node at the base, and just above a node at the top. Carefully remove all the leaves without damaging the buds, then dip the bottom end of the cutting in a rooting powder or solution. These cuttings are now ready for planting in a prepared position outside. When doing so, make sure that only one-third of the cuttings are above ground, otherwise too much drying out will occur. Rooted cuttings will be ready for transplanting to their permanent positions in November the following year.

In compiling the following A-Z lists, I have limited them to the varieties we have grown with success at Clack's Farm and can therefore recommend.

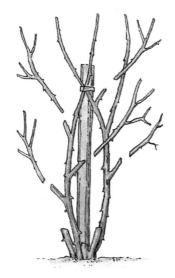

BELOW: Use sharp secateurs to make a clean cut on a slant
RIGHT: Prune climbers, and ramblers, to a framework of healthy wood
BOTTOM: Prune bush roses right down in late autumn

HYBRID TEA ROSES*

'Alec's Red': This is a sturdy medium-height grower, admirably suited to the smaller garden. The large, deep red blooms are well carried on strong upright stems and the claim that it has a sweet perfume is certainly true.

'Blessings': This great rose bred by Gregory of Nottingham, is very free flowering. We love its blooms of delicate coral salmon, which, when it decides to be generous, are produced in clusters. Being another upright grower, it is a never-fail rose for the small garden.

'Fragrant Cloud': A very popular rose that is well known for its perfume which is freely given off by its large coral-scarlet blooms. It is very free flowering and has vigorous qualities which mean it can be grown successfully on poorer soils. Its one weakness is that when the flowers age they turn dull and need dead-heading earlier than most.

'Grandpa Dickson': This is a great rose by any standard and was introduced in 1966. Its lemon-yellow blooms are often seen on the show bench but its real value is in the garden. A moderate grower, it needs a little extra attention to get the best from it and that includes its perfume.

'Josephine Bruce': For fragrance, this rose is still supreme, although it is relatively old (1949). It is well known, too, for its beautiful dark crimson velvet-like blooms, as well, unfortunately, for its susceptibility to mildew. Control the latter (see p.19) and you will love it.

'Just Joey': This is one of our favourites, and could really be called a 'poppet'. Really fragrant, especially when the air is warm, the coppery orange-red-veined blooms are beautiful. It is very free flowering and being an upright grower, easy to manage.

'Maestro': A 'hand-painted' masterpiece bred by Sam McGredy, we first saw this rose in New Zealand. The fully open blooms are an artistry of deep crimson edged with white, making it a very striking new rose. It is only a moderate grower so needs a regular feed to keep it 'on stream'.

'Mullard Jubilee': Here is a rose with robust vigour, so in consequence it needs a little more space than most. Its large rose-pink blooms are well shaped and prolific.

'National Trust': With us, this rose has never failed to go on and on producing its deep, crimson-scarlet, perfectly

'Just Joey', a beautiful bloom

shaped blooms. At all times during the growing season it remains a tidy, compact plant with strong healthy foliage. The coppery red colour of this when young adds greatly to its attraction.

'Peace': In spite of the fact that this is a variety that needs no introduction, it is still a great rose. Although its large, creamy-yellow edged and shaded pink blooms are never produced very freely, the three or four blooms produced per plant at a time still make a spectacular show. It is a vigorous grower.

'Piccadilly': This is a rose we have grown since its introduction in 1960, and with us it seems to have brushed aside such diseases as black spot and mildew. In addition it has always been generous with its scarlet and gold high-pointed buds which open to reveal the full beauty of this rose.

'Pink Favourite': One of the best bedding roses ever produced, this rose really has got everything; fragrance, large, well-shaped rose-pink blooms, plenty of healthy glossy foliage and an upright habit. It is also a good grower.

'Prima Ballerina': This is another of our favourites, bred by Tantau and introduced in 1957. A reliable grower, it makes a medium-height bush which from June onwards displays its very fragrant deep rose pink blooms. It is a good choice for a small garden.

'Whisky Mac': Another great rose from Tantau, which with us has always been a good healthy grower, never disappointing us. Its attractive deep gold blooms, with their bronze shading are perfumed and justly admired. It makes a compact bush covered with bronze-green foliage.

For growing as **standard roses** I would recommend any of the following: 'Alec's Red', 'Blessings', 'Fragrant Cloud', 'Just Joey', 'National Trust' or 'Piccadilly'.

FLORIBUNDAS*

'Arthur Bell': This is a rose that has done well with us since its introduction by Sam McGredy in 1965. Its rather large blooms, produced in trusses rather than clusters, are individually reminiscent of hybrid tea roses in their shape. These trusses of bright golden yellow roses are well perfumed and carried on strong upright stems. The dark green foliage has shown considerable resistance to disease.

'Australian Gold': We first planted this variety in 1980, since when it has proved to be a constant cropper of copious blooms with a colouring akin to ripe peaches. It is another upright grower of medium height with healthy looking dark green glossy foliage.

'Bonfire Night': A rose aptly named by Sam McGredy, as when in flower every stem carries clusters of blooms that glow with colours similar to the flames of a bonfire – a combination of orange tinged with yellow and scarlet. It is a really beautiful variety and makes a spectacular show when several are planted together.

'City of Leeds': Here is a rose introduced in 1966 by Sam McGredy which could be called a 'winner', either for mass planting or even as a single bush. With a more gla-

morous name, it may well have found the place it deserves in every rose garden. I planted 100 bushes at The Lenton Research Station in Nottingham in 1966 and every plant was still healthy and flowering well when I last saw the bed in 1981. Few new varieties have such staying powers; the delightful rich salmon blooms almost cover the plants for most of the summer.

'Elizabeth of Glamis': Right from its introduction in 1964, the name of this rose has made it extremely popular. That apart, however, it is a beautiful rose, sporting double flowers

The very popular 'Elizabeth of Glamis'

that are coral-salmon shaded with pink. On the debit side, it dislikes heavy cold clay soil situations and needs regular and careful spraying as it is less than usually resistant to disease. Lifted from the nursery with bare roots it sometimes fails to survive the transplanting. It is sensible, therefore to purchase it as a container grown plant.

'Frensham': This is the variety which will aways be associated with the advent of floribunda roses. It led the way and became immensely popular immediately after its introduction in 1946. Its masses of deep crimson blooms and its vigorous growth has a compelling appeal, which has remained in spite of its susceptibility to mildew. This must be dealt with early in the season or the disfiguring disease will run riot (see p.19).

'Iceberg': One of the finest floribunda roses ever introduced, this truly great rose from Kordes (1958) is a fairly tall grower with a parading shrub-like habit. For mass planting it is without equal and its large decorative sprays of pure white make a continuously graceful display throughout the season. The slender stems are almost devoid of thorns making it a joy at pruning time.

'Kerryman': A rose that has given great pleasure at Clack's Farm, the clusters of large hybrid tea-shaped blooms produced in various shades of pink are simply delightful. It flowers freely throughout the season and is an excellent choice for the smaller garden.

'Lili Marlene': When introduced by Kordes in 1959, this rose was an immediate success, partly because of its name and partly because of its semi-double, crimson-scarlet blooms and its compact medium-growth habit. It is a good garden rose especially for planting towards the front of a rose bed. We have found it necessary to start spraying early in the season to keep it free from mildew throughout August and September.

'Koresia': With good yellow roses still something of a rarity this one stands out as su-

'Iceberg' is a superbly free-flowering rose

perb. Here is a variety that has charmed us with its fragrance and its golden yellow blooms that appear in clusters and are of the classical hybrid tea dimensions. They are produced in quantity on the plants which grow to medium height and good shape, thus making this the type of bush that always looks tidy.

'Mary Sumner': The double copper-vermilion blooms of this rose are freely produced in well shaped trusses, and seen against the background of glossy, truly healthy foliage, they make an immediate appeal. The rose was an intro-

duction from Sam McGredy (1975); we love it and would expect to be growing it for many years to come.

'Masquerade': This was the first multi-coloured floribunda introduced by Boemer in 1949. Its blooms (like Joseph's coat of many colours) were unique at its time of introduction and made it tremendously popular. Its bright yellow buds open to reveal anything from cream to pink, moving on to crimson in the open flowers. Its ability to flower freely, its neat growth habit and above all its cheerful appearance during the summer flowering season, helps it to retain its favoured place in many gardens.

'Matangi': We regard this as one of Sam McGredy's best introductions (1974). Right from the start, it has been a healthy grower with a medium height, bushy growth habit, making it well suited for planting either singly or in quantity. Its double blooms of orange-vermilion with silver shading at the base of each petal, repeated on the reverse, are delightfully fragrant. The glow of Matangi in full bloom reminds us of the New Zealand sunset colours.

'News': We regarded the introduction of this rose as great news in 1969. Coming from Norfolk it is a robust grower and very free flowering. The deep wine red buds are most attractive, and they open to blooms that become rich purple with golden anthers.

'Regensburg': A fascinating little rose which needs encouraging to make sufficient growth when planted in a bed. It is an ideal rose for planting in a container to brighten up a patio. The double white and pink blooms with their open eyes, are a just reward for Sam McGredy and his endeavour to introduce what almost seems to be hand painting of rose petals in his roses.

'St Boniface': Another low-growing variety named by Kordes (1980) in honour of a British saint. Its perfectly shaped blooms are always a bright and cheerful vermilion. When planting choose a place at the front of the bed so that it can be seen or, alternatively, plant it in a narrow raised bed.

'Scarlet Queen Elizabeth': Bred by Dickson and introduced in 1963, this rose is not quite as tall as the more famous pink Queen Elizabeth but it is nevertheless a strong robust grower. It produces bright scarlet, semi-double blooms and has most attractive healthy bronze-green foliage. Plant it at the back of the bed or as a hedge.

'Sue Lawley': This is another 'hand-painted' rose from Sam McGredy's vintage year, 1980. Like Regensburg, it also loves that extra handful of farmyard manure. The double rosy-pink blooms with their white eyes are delightfully edged with lighter pink and white which unfortunately do tend to bleach in bright sunlight.

'Queen Elizabeth': This well known and still very popular, tall-growing rose was introduced by Lammers in 1956. Few roses can compete with the clarity of colour in its blooms, the soft, clear pink of which has won it its place in so many gardens. Give it space where its height is an advantage or plant it as a hedge and it will be a real joy. Few roses have as good a health record, every leaf shines brightly.

'Trumpeter': A rose that has been an outstanding success. From the start to finish of each season it has produced its scarlet trusses of blooms so generously, it must merit the strongest possible recommendation. In addition its short compact growth habit makes it one of the best bedding roses available at this time. It can be termed a truly great garden rose.

Some floribundas are very good for growing as standard roses. Of those listed here I would suggest: 'Iceberg', 'Koresia', 'Mary Sumner', 'Matangi' and 'Trumpeter'.

'Trumpeter', a truly glorious colour

REPEAT-FLOWERING SHRUB ROSES*

These are a real asset to any garden but generally need more space than either hybrid teas or floribundas. In a smaller garden, a single specimen is acceptable but if the garden is on the large side these shrub roses look well planted in groups of three.

'Ballerina': Makes a 1.2 metre (4 ft) shrub which, in bloom, is covered with great clusters of small single pink flowers with white eyes. Introduced by Bentall in 1937, it is a very showy rose and one of the flower arranger's favourites as it lasts well after cutting.

'Dorothy Wheatcroft': A floribunda shrub rose introduced by Tantau in 1960 that is very vigorous. It will grow up to 1.5 metres (5 ft) high on good soil. The glowing bright red single blooms are carried in large trusses and tend to be so perfect that they are often seen on the show benches with red 1st prize winners cards.

'Kerdes Robusta': As a rose we were privileged to grow before its introduction in 1982, we cannot speak too highly of this one. Grown as an individual plant it needs space in order that it may be enjoyed to the full. With us it grows to 1.5-1.8 metres (5-6 ft) and is truly vigorous, with excellent dark green foliage and some mighty strong thorns. The latter make it a variety to grow as a hedge to keep away unwanted visitors; whilst the thorns may deter the vandals the single scarlet blooms with their outstandingly beautiful golden stamens are a joy to everyone. Flowering begins early and goes on until the autumn. It really is a great rose if you have space or want to make a flowering hedge.

'Louise Odier': One of the old Bourbon roses (1851), this is a firm favourite for the flower arranger's summer creations. It has a rich pink bloom, softly shaded with a tinge of lilac and a scent that pervades the garden. It is not too vigorous a grower.

'Westerland': The bright golden orange semi-double blooms of this shrub rose are a real joy. Whilst it is vigorous in habit, it can be contained with drastic pruning and could therefore be grown in a bed.

SUMMER-FLOWERING SHRUB ROSES*

There are many different types of roses that come under this heading; the damask, moss and rose species being some of them. Only a few can be mentioned here, but any good rose catalogue will give a more extensive list.

'Fritz Nobis': One of the so-called modern hybrids, we put this at the top of our list for beauty and performance. Early in June the long pointed salmon-pink buds appear, soon to be followed by the large semi-double blooms of soft creamy pink. It is a vigorous grower easily reaching up to 1.8 metres (6 ft) or more.

'Madam Hardy': One of the damask roses we like very much, it makes a vigorous bush of medium height. The pure white blooms give out that wonderful old fashioned fragrance.

'Nuits De Young': This is a beautiful moss rose with deep blackish-purple small blooms which, when fully open, show yellow stamens. It is not too vigorous, its maximum height

'Madame Hardy', a damask rose

being about 1.2 metres (4 ft) which makes it suitable for the small town garden.

Rosa × highdownensis: This is our first choice of the rose species, and it is a vigorous grower needing plenty of space. It has deep pink single flowers, but its main attraction is its flask-shaped hips.

Rosa rubrifolia: This is without doubt our second choice. It is a much more moderate grower with dark red stems and purple grey foliage. A variety for the flower arranger, the small pink flowers are followed by bright mahogany hips. Its growth habit is best suited to the smaller garden.

CLIMBING AND RAMBLING ROSES*

'Albertine': This wonderful summer flowering climbing rose, seen at its best in June-July, was introduced by Barbier in 1921. Few roses can claim to bloom more profusely, or be more beautiful or more fragrant than Albertine. Just a single plant will add another dimension to your flower garden. The deep coppery red buds open to soft salmon-pink flowers, so numerous that they simply smother the whole plant to make a magnificent display which lasts for fully a month.

Altissimo': This is a really vigorous climber which will make 4.5 metres (15 ft) or more growth without much encouragement. Its dark green foliage clearly displays its health and vigour and, given a chance, it will go on flowering throughout the whole season. Seen against a brickwork background the single large flowers with their golden stamens are indeed glorious.

'American Pillar': Still grown

'Albertine' is a prolific climber

and popular although introduced as long ago as 1902 by Van Fleet, this is a vigorous rambler appreciated for its bright cerise pink, white-centred flowers which are at their peak in June and July. It is a variety that is often planted and then forgotten, but it does so much better when it is given an occasional feed with a rose fertiliser.

'Danse Du Feu': This is a climber that can be grown against a north wall although it does somewhat better in more sunny situations. A vigorous grower – reaching up to 4.5 metres (15 ft) – it is capable of making a fine show throughout the season with its semi-double, bright orange-red blooms and glossy dark green foliage. It is a great rose for the front of the house.

'Dreaming Spires': This rose is a 1973 Mattock introduction of fairly vigorous habit. The bright golden blooms have a delightful fragrance and are shown up by its heavy dark green foliage. If given that extra dose of fertiliser, it will flower through the summer.

'Galway Bay': A climbing rose from Sam McGredy which was introduced in 1966, it has a growth habit which makes it suitable for training as a pillar rose rather than up against a wall. From June onwards it produces its cerise pink blooms generously.

'Golden Showers': A rose we love, this one will suffer all sorts of treatment and still come up with its bright yellow blooms in profusion throughout the whole season. As a climber it is excellent, even on a north wall, and it will go to a height of 1.8 metres (6 ft). Restrained by pruning and treated as a shrub, it is still happy if the soil is good.

'Handel': One of our finest climbers (Sam McGredy 1965), this rose grows up to 3 metres (10 ft). There can be few more beautiful sights in a garden than an established Handel in full bloom with its creamy-white suffused roses edged with bright rose-pink. The half open blooms are of medium size and near perfectly shaped. It is no wonder that it is so popular either as a climber or as a restricted growth shrub rose.

'Mermaid': Once established this rose is very vigorous but it may sulk for a year or two after planting before deciding it likes and will accept the position in your garden. Once settled in a spot with plenty of room, it produces large, single, pale sulphur yellow flowers with amber stamens that are unbelievably beautiful. No other climber has such glossy foliage.

'Park Direktor Riggers': A very clean, vigorous and large grower introduced by Kordes in 1957, this rose has plenty of strong wood to cover a house wall. It then adorns it with super brilliant crimson, semi-double blooms in large clusters, set off by beautiful glossy dark green foliage. I have never known anyone to be disappointed with it.

'Pink Perpetue': This is a variety greatly admired by visitors to Clack's Farm. Planted on the south-facing wall of our house it starts to flower to-

'Zephirine Drouhin' is a thornless climber

wards the end of May and goes on producing its bright rose pink with salmon-rose shades blooms until the autumn. Already our two plants have exceeded 3 metres (10 ft) and have every appearance of growing higher still.

'Wedding Day': This is a true summer flowering rambler, suitable for growing into trees and over tall archways. The buds are yellow but open to white flowers with a rich fragrance.

'Zephirine Drouhin': The thornless climber introduced way back in 1868 by Bizot, which was almost lost until seen on television growing in the Royal National Rose Society's trial grounds at St. Albans. Now it is a great favourite with those who know how to control its mildew problems. Its glorious carmine pink blooms are delightfully fragrant and it will flower continuously throughout the whole season.

All these climbers, ramblers and true shrub roses produce their flowers on the previous season's wood, so in consequ-

ence they are not likely to flower in their first year after planting. Do remember this when pruning; leave some new growth otherwise there will be few roses on the plants the following season.

MINIATURE ROSES*

Whilst some of the miniature roses are recommended for open ground planting, my own experience with them indicates that while they do produce charming miniature blooms, practically all exceed their catalogue heights even during their first year outdoors. However there is undoubtedly a place for them in containers or pots where root restriction has a considerable effect on the size of the plant. A patio or balcony is the obvious place for them.

'Baby Masquerade': A charming small bush with multi-coloured miniature yellow, pink and red flowers right through the summer.

'Dresden Doll': This is the star of them all with its miniature shell-pink moss roses. They start as tiny buds covered with

The miniature 'Baby Masquerade'

growth that looks like light green moss. Later they open into small, fully double blooms making it a most charming plant.

In this same category come the **ground cover roses**, so called because their spread is greater than their height.

'Nozomi': A dainty ground cover rose with small pale pink single flowers in large clusters. It will grow to a height of 30-45 cm (12-18 inches) and is very effective when grown in a tall container or where it has the opportunity to trail down.

'Snow Carpet': Bred by Sam McGredy (1980). We have found that after three years at Clack's Farm each plant covers almost a square metre (just over a square yard) but its height has continued to remain under 20 cm (8 inches). Its foliage is dark green throughout the season when much of the time the plants are covered with tiny snow-white double miniature roses.

INDEX